The U.S. War on Drugs at Home and Abroad

Jonathan D. Rosen

The U.S. War on Drugs at Home and Abroad

Jonathan D. Rosen
Holy Family University
Philadelphia, PA, USA

ISBN 978-3-030-71733-9   ISBN 978-3-030-71734-6 (eBook)
https://doi.org/10.1007/978-3-030-71734-6

© The Author(s), under exclusive licence to Springer Nature Switzerland AG 2021
This work is subject to copyright. All rights are solely and exclusively licensed by the Publisher, whether the whole or part of the material is concerned, specifically the rights of translation, reprinting, reuse of illustrations, recitation, broadcasting, reproduction on microfilms or in any other physical way, and transmission or information storage and retrieval, electronic adaptation, computer software, or by similar or dissimilar methodology now known or hereafter developed.
The use of general descriptive names, registered names, trademarks, service marks, etc. in this publication does not imply, even in the absence of a specific statement, that such names are exempt from the relevant protective laws and regulations and therefore free for general use.
The publisher, the authors and the editors are safe to assume that the advice and information in this book are believed to be true and accurate at the date of publication. Neither the publisher nor the authors or the editors give a warranty, expressed or implied, with respect to the material contained herein or for any errors or omissions that may have been made. The publisher remains neutral with regard to jurisdictional claims in published maps and institutional affiliations.

Cover pattern © Harvey Loake

This Palgrave Macmillan imprint is published by the registered company Springer Nature Switzerland AG.
The registered company address is: Gewerbestrasse 11, 6330 Cham, Switzerland

To Karina Castillo—Thanks for making me a better person.

Acknowledgments

I would like to thank Palgrave Macmillan for this wonderful opportunity. It has been a true honor to work with this publishing house. In addition, I would like to thank two anonymous peer reviewers. Their comments helped improve the quality of this manuscript.

A special thanks to Hanna Kassab, Deborah Rosen Evans, and Sebastián Cutrona for their comments and edits. My research assistants, Jessica Holzworth and Brianna Pudlo, also provided excellent comments.

Last but not least, I would like to thank Karina Castillo for always pushing me to be better. A special thanks for believing in me and supporting my academic dreams.

Contents

1 Introduction — 1

2 The Drug War in Colombia — 17

3 Drug Trafficking and Organized Crime in Mexico — 45

4 Addiction, Fentanyl, and the Border — 75

5 Prisons and the Consequences of Tough on Crime Policies at Home and Abroad — 97

6 Conclusion — 123

Selected Work Cited — 137

Index — 145

List of Figures

Fig. 2.1 United States funding for plan Colombia (in millions of dollars). (Source: Created by author with data from June S. Beittel and Claire Ribando Seelke, *Colombia: Issues for Congress* (Washington, DC: Congressional Research Service, 2009); State Department Foreign Operations Congressional Budget Justifications; FY2006 Foreign Operations Appropriations Act, P.L. 109–102, and conference report, H.Rept. 109–265)   25

Fig. 2.2 Kidnappings in Colombia during the Uribe administration. (Source: Created by author with data from Washington Office on Latin America, 15th *Anniversary of Plan Colombia: Learning from Its Successes and Failures* (Washington, DC: WOLA, 2016); Ministry of Defense of Colombia)   27

Fig. 2.3 Colombian's perceptions about the likelihood of the FARC stopping drug trafficking after a peace agreement. (Source: Created by author with LAPOP 2016/2017 data)   31

Fig. 2.4 Coca cultivation in Colombia (in hectares). (Source: Created by author with data from United Nations Office on Drugs and Crime (UNODC), *Colombia: Monitoreo de territorios afectados por cultivos ilícitos 2017* (Bogotá, CO: Colombia, 2018))   33

Fig. 3.1 Number of deaths in Mexico (2013–2017). (Source: Created by author with data from *Proceso*)   55

Fig. 3.2 2016/2017 Survey response to level of protection for human rights in Mexico Today. (Source: Created by author with data from LAPOP 2016/2017)   59

Fig. 4.1   2017 Age-adjusted death rate per 100,000. (Source: Created by author with data from 2017 Drug Overdose Death Rates, Center for Disease Control and Prevention)   79

Fig. 4.2   Number of deaths from drug overdose (2017). (Source: Created by author with data from 2017 Number of Drug Overdose Deaths, Center for Disease Control and Prevention)   80

Fig. 4.3   Nationwide drug seizures of fentanyl between FY 2016-FY 2020 (in pounds). (Source: Created by author with data from "CBP Enforcement Statistics Fiscal Year 2020," U.S. Customs and Border Protection)   87

Fig. 5.1   Total number of people serving life sentences. (Source: The Sentencing Project, *Fact Sheet: Trends in U.S. Corrections* (Washington, DC: The Sentencing Project, 2019); A. Nellis, *Still Life: America's Increasing Use of Life and Long-Term Sentences* (Washington, DC: The Sentencing Project, 2016))   101

CHAPTER 1

Introduction

Abstract This chapter provides a brief history of the war on drugs. It analyzes the policy proposals of the Richard Nixon administration, which launched the war on drugs in 1971, to the Donald Trump administration. This chapter also highlights the objectives of this book. It seeks to provide a brief guide to the war on drugs at home and abroad. The work is not heavy on theory and methodology but rather seeks to be accessible to students, experts, and policymakers looking to learn more about this subject. This chapter also justifies the case selection and provides an overview of the book.

Keywords War on drugs • Drug trafficking • Richard Nixon • Policy • History • Case selection

You pick up your favorite newspaper and the front-page cover story is about a Mexican drug cartel killing many innocent bystanders during a shootout. You have been following what has been transpiring in Mexico, which has caused the deaths of hundreds of thousands of people over the past decade.[1] You start to question whether the "war on drugs" can ever be won. It has been estimated that the United States has spent over one trillion dollars on the war on drugs since Nixon launched this war in the 1970s. Despite spending billions of dollars per year combating drugs at home and abroad, drugs remain more readily available than ever before.[2]

© The Author(s), under exclusive license to Springer Nature Switzerland AG 2021
J. D. Rosen, *The U.S. War on Drugs at Home and Abroad*, https://doi.org/10.1007/978-3-030-71734-6_1

The U.S.-led war on drugs has focused so much on stopping the supply of drugs from entering the United States, yet the United States remains the number one drug-consuming country in the world. Just like any other commodity, drugs are produced and trafficked because the demand for drugs exists.[3] Today, drugs are more readily available than when the war on drugs began.[4]

While one might assume that the people who are being arrested and sentenced to jail or prison for drug-related charges are major drug kingpins, the reality is that millions of people have been arrested and served time in jail or prison for non-violent drug offenses. The United States has continued its tough on crime policies against individuals who have committed drug violations. Authorities have arrested more than 1.429 million people for the possession of drugs. In 2016, for example, the United States incarcerated more than 450,000 people for violating drug laws. In 2018, police arrested 663,367 individuals for breaking marijuana drug laws.[5]

The number of people sentenced for drug-related crimes has increased over time. Half of the people in federal prisons (i.e., people who have been convicted of breaking federal laws in the United States) are incarcerated for drug-related offenses. While some experts emphasize the fact that most prisoners are not in federal prisons but rather state facilities,[6] the federal inmate population is still substantial. In 1980, for example, 4749 of the 22,037 people in federal prisons received sentences for drug-related charges. By 1995, the government sentenced 52,782 of the 88,658 prisoners in federal prison for drug charges. By 2010, the number of people in federal prisons for drug-related charges increased to 97,800, while the total prison population was 186,545.[7]

Having a criminal record is often very problematic for people trying to apply for jobs and universities because people who are arrested are often labeled as troublemakers and have a red flag next to their record. Said differently, it is hard enough to find employment and much harder if you have a criminal record because employers label you and are hesitant to hire people with a criminal history. The situation is even worse when somebody is arrested for a felony. A felony, by definition, is a crime that is punishable by incarceration for a year or more, as opposed to a misdemeanor which is less than a year. People with felonies on their record are denied public housing and continue to be punished even after serving their sentences. Felons are also not permitted to vote in many states. Finally, people with felony convictions often are stigmatized and shunned by the community.[8]

Brief History of the War on Drugs

Some experts contend that the United States has had a drug war for more than 100 years with the passage of the Harrison Narcotics Tax Act of 1914, which regulated the sales of opioids as well as cocaine. Various laws regulated marijuana, such as the 1937 Marijuana Tax Act, the 1952 Boggs Acts, and the 1956 Narcotics Control Act.[9]

In 1971, President Richard Nixon argued that drug abuse constituted "public enemy number one." Nixon maintained that combating this threat required a "new, all-out offense," and his administration officially declared a "war on drugs."[10] Nixon asserted that the government needed to stop the supply as well as the demand. He contended, "I am convinced that the only way to fight this menace is by attacking it on many fronts."[11] Nixon asked Congress to fund $155 million more in the budget for drug abuse.[12]

Some experts argue that the "enthusiasm" with which the Nixon administration sought to combat drugs was related to heroin usage by soldiers in Vietnam.[13] Many soldiers suffered from Post-Traumatic Stress Disorder (PTSD) and did not receive the proper treatment to address these traumas. As a result, some soldiers used drugs as a coping mechanism to ease their pain and suffering from the events that they witnessed during the war. Nixon addressed this issue, stating:

> Fundamentally, it is essential for the American people to be alerted to this danger, to recognize that it is a danger that will not pass with the passing of the war in Vietnam which has brought to our attention the fact that a number of young Americans have become addicts as they serve abroad, whether in Vietnam, or Europe, or other places. Because the problem existed before we became involved in Vietnam; it will continue to exist afterwards. That is why this offensive deals with the problem.[14]

The efforts to combat drug consumption and production also led the Nixon administration to create the Drug Enforcement Administration (DEA) in 1973.[15]

The second major drug epidemic occurred in the 1980s with widespread use of cocaine. Powdered cocaine is quite expensive and became popular among some affluent Americans. Cocaine has been referred to as a "party" drug because people use it at nightclubs. The 1980s witnessed the "crack boom," particularly in the inner cities, as crack is a much cheaper form of this substance. This epidemic had a devastating impact on many Americans, particularly people living in marginalized communities. Ronald Reagan launched the modern phase of the drug war, viewing these substances as evil. He believed that drugs were eroding the moral values of Americans and destroying families.[16]

President Ronald Reagan's wife, Nancy, launched her "Just Say No" campaign in 1981, and the administration escalated the drug war by implementing zero-tolerance policies.[17] In 1986, President Reagan elevated drugs on the security agenda when he issued a presidential directive that made drug trafficking a threat to U.S. national security. The directive provided the intelligence community and the department of defense with the authority to become more involved in initiatives designed to combat drug trafficking and prevent drugs from crossing into the United States.[18]

The Reagan administration's drug war policies were based on fear and had a direct impact on the number of people incarcerated for drug-related crimes.[19] The death of Len Bias, a basketball player at the University of Maryland, who died of a drug overdose after he was picked by the Boston Celtics, sparked fear and countless media stories. It was alleged that Bias died from an overdose of crack cocaine. The U.S. Congress acted quickly and passed the Anti-Drug Abuse Act of 1986 only several weeks after the death of Bias. The U.S. government wanted to combat the crack cocaine epidemic. As this book will argue in the other chapters, fear and anger should not drive public policy. The Anti-Drug Abuse Act of 1986 created a large discrepancy between people who consumed or sold crack cocaine. Prior to the passage of the Fair Sentencing Act of 2010, a 100 to 1 disparity existed for crack cocaine versus powder cocaine,[20] even though these are the same drug—the only difference is who uses the drug and how they use it.[21]

Yet Republican politicians are not the only ones who have implemented the drug war and tough on crime policies. The Bill Clinton administration, for example, has been criticized for its tough on crime policies. As will be discussed in the chapter on prisons, the Clinton administration's 1994 Crime Bill contributed to a massive increase in the prison population. The Clinton government did not seek to address the disparities between sentencing for powder versus crack cocaine, which contributed to the racial disparities for drug sentencing.

The Clinton administration also supported counternarcotic initiatives abroad, such as Plan Colombia, which focused on reducing drug production and trafficking in Colombia. Critics of the Clinton government maintain that these counternarcotic plans did not address the underlying issues that contribute to drug trafficking and organized crime. The role of domestic politics in the United States also helps explain the support for Plan Colombia. The original plan sought to decrease the cultivation of coca as well as the production and trafficking of drugs.[22] This bipartisan initiative helped President Clinton refute Republican critics who labeled him as someone who was "soft on crime." President Clinton had been criticized previously for not doing more to combat crime and violence at home and abroad. Plan Colombia represented an initiative that he could point to about how his administration took combating drug trafficking and organized crime seriously.[23]

The war on drugs evolved during the George W. Bush administration, which focused on foreign policy and national security after the terrorist attacks on September 11, 2001. As will be discussed in the chapter on Colombia, the Bush administration focused on combating terrorism around the globe. This led to a fusion of the war on drugs with the war on terror.[24] Skeptics of the Bush administration contend that it focused too much on the militarization of the drug war and combating the supply of drugs. While advocates of initiatives like Plan Colombia maintain that it increased security in Colombia, critics contend that the plan did not reduce the production and trafficking of drugs.

The election of Barack Obama in 2008 to the presidency provided hope among people who favored an end to the prohibitionist policies that have cost the United States billions of dollars and systematically ruined the lives of many people, many of whom have been arrested, jailed, and imprisoned for drug-related charges. The Obama administration ended the rhetoric of the war on drugs in 2009.[25] The administration argued that the term "war on drugs" makes it sound as though it is a war against individuals. President Obama emphasized the need to treat drugs as a public health issue. The Obama government even proposed the first drug control budget since Jimmy Carter that would allocate more resources to public health than law enforcement and other agencies focusing on combating the supply of drugs.[26]

Furthermore, President Obama commuted hundreds of people for drug-related charges. The chapter on prisons analyzes several cases of people who had their sentences commuted by the president. Obama's policies, including clemencies, enabled him to decrease the federal prison population by the end of his time in office. Yet some individuals maintain that he could have commuted more and done it faster.[27]

Colorado and Washington legalized marijuana in 2012, and the Obama administration vowed not to use federal resources to prosecute users in these states. Critics argued that President Obama did not do enough to change the drug war policies. Advocates of marijuana legalization criticized Obama for not supporting legalization. Critics also maintained that law enforcement officials arrested hundreds of thousands of people for violating marijuana laws each year. Some advocates for drug policy reform argued that the Obama administration could have made more progress in rolling back some of the punitive drug laws and focused less on law enforcement initiatives.[28]

The Trump administration rolled back many of the reforms of the Obama government. President Donald Trump ran for president on a law-and-order platform and vowed to "Make America Great Again." He harped against the "weak" immigration policies of his predecessor and contended that drugs are pouring over the border from Mexico. Trump stated many times during his campaign rallies that the United States needs to protect its border and is a country of laws.[29]

President Trump appointed Jeff Sessions as his Attorney General. Sessions has a long history of conservative policies, particularly regarding immigration and the war on drugs. Attorney General Sessions made critical comments against marijuana laws and indicated that he would enforce the federal drug laws. Sessions argued, "[M]arijuana is against federal law, and that applies in states where they may have repealed their own anti-marijuana laws."[30] It is possible that federal authorities could arrest someone living in a state where marijuana is legal for violating federal drug laws. This, in turn, would likely result in that individual filing a lawsuit, which could move through the state system and eventually would have to be decided at the United States' Supreme Court.[31] This issue has even divided conservatives, who tend to focus on states' rights.

The Trump administration ramped up the war on drugs. During his time in office, Sessions instructed prosecutors to seek the maximum sentence for people who violated the law. According to Sessions, "This policy fully utilizes the tools Congress has given us. The most serious offenses are those that carry the most substantial guidelines sentence, including mandatory-minimum sentences."[32] The emphasis on mandatory minimum sentencing has flooded the prison system with non-violent offenders. A return to prosecutors seeking the maximum penalties could lead to a spike in the already overflowing prison population.

Furthermore, President Trump touted the drug war on the global scale. In 2018, he noted that more than 100 countries signed onto a call to renew the global drug war, known as a "Global Call to Action on the World Drug Problem." Critics, however, contended that this call to action was reverting to the failed drug war policies that have not been effective for decades. According to John Walsh of the Washington Office on Latin America (WOLA), "The U.S. is trying to lead us backwards now to the failed policies that led us here."[33] The Trump administration returned to a focus on supply-side strategies despite the countless academic and policy studies that exist indicating that these policies have not been effective. The Trump administration, therefore, moved away from the desire by many presidents around the globe to change the drug war strategies.

Objectives of This Book

The goal of this book is to provide a brief overview of the U.S. war on drugs at home and abroad. It is intended for people who are interested in a brief—the keyword being brief—summary of some of the trends in the U.S. war on drugs. I had the idea for writing this book as I not only teach on transnational organized crime, the drug war, and the prison system, but also have given lectures throughout the Americas on drug trafficking, organized crime, and violence to different audiences. I have published several large volumes on drug trafficking and organized crime that are designed for academics.[34] While several hundred-page volumes by scholars can be very useful and provide excellent information, I want this book to be a short—and hopefully fun—read about some of the major events in the war on drugs. This book, therefore, is not designed to be a comprehensive guide to the U.S.-led war on drugs around the globe. For people interested in learning more about the topics discussed in this work, I have provided many scholarly sources in the endnotes.

While this work is designed to help readers think about different policy issues, it is not heavy on theory and methodology. There are many books in criminal justice, political science, sociology, anthropology, and other disciplines that focus on U.S. foreign policy, drug trafficking, and organized crime. Many of these works are designed for academics and have a strong theoretical foundation. There are also both quantitative and qualitative works on crime, drugs, prisons, and various other topics. Some of these studies require a background in methodology and can be hard to access given the complicated statistical models run by scholars.[35] While I have conducted both quantitative, qualitative, and mixed-method research in other academic publications, this book is not focused on methodology.[36] I wrote this book with the goal of making it jargon-free and not laden with theory and methods. The book, however, is data-driven and has some graphs to explain trends in drug policy and corrections. Yet I decided not to run regression models as my goal in writing this book is to have it appeal to a broad audience. I encourage readers who are interested in the theoretical and methodological debates to peruse the endnotes and read the scholarly works cited there.

Case Selection and Approach

The book focuses on the war on drugs at home as well as U.S. policies in Colombia and Mexico. One may ask why I decided to focus on Colombia and Mexico. Indeed, this is not an exhaustive list of the countries where the U.S. government has supported counternarcotic policies. There are various works that discuss the drug war in the Andean Region and other areas around the globe.[37]

This book focuses on Colombia and Mexico because the U.S. government has invested billions of dollars combating drug trafficking and organized crime in these countries. Critics maintain that there has been a militarization of the war on drugs, which has fueled violence.[38] Despite initiatives like Plan Colombia and the Mérida Initiative, which focused on reducing drug trafficking and organized crime, these problems have continued unabated. Colombia remains the leading producer of cocaine entering the United States today. The country has seen a changing criminal landscape in the emergence of more criminal actors. While Mexico has not historically been a major drug producer, it is a transit country. The war on drugs in Mexico has been supported by the U.S. government. Mexico has seen hundreds of thousands of drug-related deaths over the past 14 years. Mexico has also experienced a fragmentation of organized crime, and dozens of powerful criminal groups compete for control of trafficking routes and territory.[39]

This book also focuses on the intricate linkage between the war on drugs, addiction, and the U.S.-Mexico border. The argument is that there is an intricate connection between the drug war and the prison population. In the United States and other Latin American countries, the prison populations have spiked because of tough on crime policies. There are many scholars who have written about the prison system in the United States.[40] This book argues that the prison system requires systematic reforms. The prison population in the United States has proliferated over time and costs taxpayers billions of dollars. This book analyzes the trends in U.S. corrections and focuses on various Latin American cases. Other countries have even received U.S. government funding to reform their prisons and have often turned to the United States as a model.

Book Overview

Chapter 2 examines drug trafficking, organized crime, and violence in Colombia, which has been a focal point of the U.S.-led war on drugs for many years as this country not only has been a producer of coca but also has cocaine traffickers. This chapter begins with an examination of the linkages between Miami and Colombia, emphasizing the "cocaine connection." It then examines the major players in organized crime in Colombia during the 1980s and early 1990s, focusing on the Medellín and Cali cartels. It then turns to Plan Colombia, a multi-billion-dollar initiative designed to combat drug trafficking and organized crime. This chapter analyzes how Plan Colombia evolved during the Pastrana and Uribe administrations and the Clinton and Bush governments. It then assesses the evolution of organized crime and the emergence of new criminal bands and a new generation of drug traffickers. It concludes with an analysis of the Duque administration, which has witnessed increasing levels of coca production and has faced pressure from the Trump administration to reduce drug production and trafficking.

Chapter 3 analyzes drug trafficking and organized crime in Mexico. This chapter begins by examining the intricate relationship between drug traffickers and one political party, which dominated the political landscape for more than seven decades until the transition to democracy in 2000. It then examines how the transition to democracy created an environment ripe for drug trafficking and organized crime, given the high levels of corruption and impunity. This chapter then turns to the Calderón administration's war on drugs, which the Bush government supported through the Mérida Initiative. It highlights the consequences of such strategies, including the fragmentation of organized crime and increasing levels of violence. It then focuses on the Enrique Peña Nieto administration and analyzes trends in organized crime and violence. This chapter also addresses the challenges that President Andrés Manuel López Obrador confronts as he inherited a country that faces major obstacles with corruption, impunity, and rising levels of violence.

Chapter 4 begins with an examination of the opioid epidemic in the United States. It focuses on the role of major pharmaceutical companies and highlights the issue of overprescribing by some doctors. This chapter describes different stories of addiction. It then turns to the case of fentanyl, focusing on trends in consumption. It highlights the case of Philadelphia and the Kensington neighborhood, which has become an epicenter of opioid trafficking and consumption. Kensington has seen the presence of both fentanyl and carfentanil, which is even more powerful and dangerous than fentanyl. This chapter examines the efforts by a non-profit organization to start the nation's first safe injection site in Philadelphia. It then examines the supply-chain of fentanyl and the debate over President Trump's border wall.

Chapter 5 focuses on the prison system in the Americas. It begins with an examination of the events that led to the passage of the 1994 Crime Bill. This chapter assesses trends in corrections, including the costs and the total number of people behind bars. It highlights not only the racial disparities but also the increasing number of women incarcerated for drug-related crimes. It focuses on some of the underlying factors, which make it difficult for former inmates to reinsert themselves into society. This chapter then turns to the prison system in Latin America. It shows that the tough on crime policies have led to increases in the prison populations. It concludes by examining the importance of understanding the needs of prison populations in the Americas.

Chapter 6 serves as the concluding chapter of this book. It focuses on the need to reduce the demand for drugs. It stresses the need to base policy decisions on science. It argues that data-driven approaches should lead any policy discussion, as opposed to fear and anger. This chapter highlights the importance of focusing on context and the lessons learned from past policy failures. It also underlines the importance of comprehensive reforms to address corruption and impunity, which have enabled drug traffickers to thrive in some countries in the Americas.

Notes

1. Ted Galen Carpenter, *The Fire Next Door: Mexico's Drug Violence and the Danger to America*, (Washington, D.C.: Cato Institute, 2012); Charles Bowden, *Murder City: Ciudad Juárez and the global economy's new killing fields* (New York, NY: Nation Books, 2010); Charles Bowden, *Juárez: The laboratory of our future* (New York, NY: Aperture, 1998).
2. Drug Policy Alliance, "Forty Years of Failure," *DPA*, http://www.drugpolicy.org/new-solutions-drug-policy/forty-years-failure, accessed June 23, 2020. For more on the war on drugs in the Americas, see Bruce M. Bagley, ed. *Drug Trafficking Research in the Americas* (Coral Gables, FL: University of Miami, North-South Center, 1997); see Bruce M. Bagley and William O. Walker III, eds., *Drug-Trafficking in the Americas* (Coral Gables, FL: University of Miami, North-South Center, 1994); Russell Crandall, *Driven by Drugs* (Boulder, Colo: Lynne Rienner, 2002).
3. Ethan A. Nadelmann, "Thinking Seriously about Alternatives to Drug Prohibition," *Daedalus* 121, no. 31 (1992): pp. 85–85; United Nations Office on Drugs and Crime (UNODC), *World Drug Report, 2011* (New York, NY: UNODC, 2011).
4. Bruce M. Bagley and Jonathan D. Rosen, eds., *Drug Trafficking, Organized Crime, and Violence in the Americas Today* (Gainesville, FL: University Press of Florida, 2015).
5. For more, see: Drug Policy Alliance (DPA), "Drug War Statistics," *DPA*, https://www.drugpolicy.org/issues/drug-war-statistics, accessed June 29, 2020.
6. John Pfaff, *Locked In: The True Causes of Mass Incarceration-and How to Achieve Real Reform* (New York, NY: Basic Books, 2017).
7. The Sentencing Project, *Fact Sheet: Trends in U.S. Corrections* (Washington, DC: The Sentencing Project, 2019).
8. Michelle Alexander, *The New Jim Crow: Mass Incarceration in the Age of Colorblindness* (New York, NY: The New Press, 2010), p. 146.
9. Marten W. Brienen and Jonathan D. Rosen, "Introduction," in *New Approaches to Drug Policies: A Time For Change*, eds. Marten W. Brienen and Jonathan D. Rosen (New York, NY: Palgrave Macmillan, 2015): pp. 1–13; Bruce Michael Bagley, "The new hundred years war? US national security and the war on drugs in Latin America," *Journal of Interamerican Studies and World Affairs* 30, no. 1 (1988): pp. 161–182; David F. Musto, *The American disease: Origins of narcotic control* (New York, NY: Oxford University Press, 1999).
10. Chris Barber, "Public Enemy Number One: A Pragmatic Approach to America's Drug Problem," *Richard Nixon Foundation*, June 29, 2016,

https://www.nixonfoundation.org/2016/06/26404/, accessed June 29, 2020.
11. Quoted in Ed Vulliamy, "Nixon's 'war on drugs' began 40 years ago, and the battle is still raging," The Guardian, July 23, 2011.
12. For the transcript, see: "Transcript of Richard Nixon's War on Drugs Speech on June 17, 1971," http://media.avvosites.com/upload/sites/396/2019/07/Transcript-of-Richard-Nixon%E2%80%99s-War-on-Drugs-Speech-on-June-17-1971-Google-Docs.pdf, accessed June 29, 2020.
13. Marten W. Brienen and Jonathan D. Rosen, "Introduction," in *New Approaches to Drug Policies: A Time For Change*, eds. Marten W. Brienen and Jonathan D. Rosen (New York, NY: Palgrave Macmillan, 2015): pp. 1–13; Christopher M. White, *The War on Drugs in the Americas* (New York, NY: Routledge, 2019).
14. "Transcript of Richard Nixon's War on Drugs Speech on June 17, 1971," http://media.avvosites.com/upload/sites/396/2019/07/Transcript-of-Richard-Nixon%E2%80%99s-War-on-Drugs-Speech-on-June-17-1971-Google-Docs.pdf, accessed June 29, 2020.
15. For more, see: Carlos A. Pérez Ricart, "The Role of the DEA in the Emergence of the Field of Anti-narcotics Policing in Latin America," *Global Governance: A Review of Multilateralism and International Organizations* 24, no. 2 (2018): pp. 169–192; María Celia Toro, "The internationalization of police: The DEA in Mexico," *The Journal of American History* 86, no. 2 (1999): pp. 623–640; Carlos A. Pérez Ricart, "Taking the War on Drugs Down South: The Drug Enforcement Administration in Mexico (1973–1980)," *The Social History of Alcohol and Drugs* 34, no. 1 (2020): pp. 82–113.
16. Bruce M. Bagley, "Drug-Control Policies in the United States: Patterns, Prevalence, and Problems of Drugs Use in the United States," pp. 121–136.
17. Drug Policy Alliance (DPA), "A Brief History of the Drug War," *DPA*, https://www.drugpolicy.org/issues/brief-history-drug-war, accessed June 29, 2020; Matthew D. Lassiter, "Impossible criminals: the suburban imperatives of America's war on drugs," *Journal of American History* 102, no. 1 (2015): pp. 126–140; James A. Inciardi, *The war on drugs: Heroin, cocaine, crime, and public policy* Vol. 1 (Palo Alto, CA: Mayfield Publishing Company, 1986).
18. Ted Galen Carpenter, "Collateral Damage: The Wide-Ranging Consequences of America's Drug War," *CATO*, https://www.cato.org/sites/cato.org/files/pictures/drugwarevent/carpenter.html, accessed June 29, 2020; James E. Hawdon, "The role of presidential rhetoric in the creation of a moral panic: Reagan, Bush, and the war on drugs," *Deviant Behavior* 22, no. 5 (2001): pp. 419–445; Bruce Michael Bagley, "US

foreign policy and the war on drugs: Analysis of a policy failure," *Journal of Interamerican Studies and World Affairs* 30, no. 2/3 (1988): pp. 189–212.
19. Drug Policy Alliance (DPA), "A Brief History of the Drug War."
20. For more, see: Carl L. Hart, Margaret Haney, Suzanne K. Vosburg, Eric Rubin, and Richard W. Foltin, "Smoked cocaine self-administration is decreased by modafinil," *Neuropsychopharmacology* 33, no. 4 (2008): pp. 761–768; Carl L. Hart, Mark Haney, R. W. Foltin, and M. W. Fischman, "Alternative reinforcers differentially modify cocaine self-administration by humans," *Behavioural Pharmacology* 11, no. 1 (2000): pp. 87–91; Edward F. Pace-Schott, Peter T. Morgan, Robert T. Malison, Carl L. Hart, Chris Edgar, Matthew Walker, and Robert Stickgold, "Cocaine users differ from normals on cognitive tasks which show poorer performance during drug abstinence," *The American Journal of Drug and Alcohol Abuse* 34, no. 1 (2008): pp. 109–121; Richard W. Foltin, Amie S. Ward, Margaret Haney, Carl L. Hart, and Eric D. Collins, "The effects of escalating doses of smoked cocaine in humans," *Drug and Alcohol Dependence* 70, no. 2 (2003): pp. 149–157.
21. American Civil Liberties Union (ACLU), "Fair Sentencing Act," https://www.aclu.org/issues/criminal-law-reform/drug-law-reform/fair-sentencing-act, accessed May 21, 2020; Philip Oliss, "Mandatory minimum sentencing: Discretion, the safety valve, and the sentencing guidelines," *University of Cincinnati Law Review* 63 (1994): p. 1851; Shimica Gaskins, "Women of Circumstance-The Effects of Mandatory Minimum Sentencing on Women Minimally Involved in Drug Crimes," *American Criminal Law Review* 41 (2004): p. 1533; William D. Bales and Linda G. Dees, "Mandatory minimum sentencing in Florida: Past trends and future implications," *Crime & Delinquency* 38, no. 3 (1992): pp. 309–329; Robert S. Mueller, "Mandatory minimum sentencing," *Federal Sentencing Reporter* 4, no. 4 (1992): pp. 230–233.
22. For more on Plan Colombia, see: Justin Delacour, "Plan Colombia: Rhetoric, Reality, and the Press," *Social Justice* 27, no. 4 82 (2000): pp. 63–75; William Avilés, "US intervention in Colombia: the role of transnational relations," *Bulletin of Latin American Research* 27, no. 3 (2008): pp. 410–429; Juan Gabriel Tokatlian, "El plan Colombia:¿ un modelo de intervención?" *Revista CIDOB d'afers internacionals* (2001): pp. 203–219; Andrew Miller, "Point: US Millitary Support for Plan Colombia: Adding Fuel to the Fire," *Human Rights Brief* 8, no. 1 (2000): p. 3; Arlene B. Tickner, "Colombia and the United States: From counter-narcotics to counterterrorism," *Current History* 102, no. 661 (2003): p. 77.
23. For more, see: Bill McCollum, "The struggle for effective anti-crime legislation-An analysis of the violent crime control and law enforcement act of

1994," *University Dayton Law Review* 20 (1994): p. 561; Tony G. Poveda, "Clinton, crime, and the justice department," *Social Justice* 21, no. 3 57 (1994): pp. 73–84.
24. For more, see: Emma Björnehed, "Narco-terrorism: The merger of the war on drugs and the war on terror," *Global Crime* 6, no. 3–4 (2004): pp. 305–324; Ingrid Vaicius and Adam Isacson, "The 'war on drugs' meets the 'war on terror,'" *International Policy Report* 2, no. 6 (2003): pp. 1–27.
25. Gary Fields, "White House Czar Calls for End to 'War on Drugs,'" *The Wall Street Journal*, May 14, 2009.
26. German Lopez, "How Obama quietly reshaped America's war on drugs," *VOX*, January 19, 2017.
27. German Lopez, "How Obama quietly reshaped America's war on drugs," *VOX*, January 19, 2017.
28. German Lopez, "How Obama quietly reshaped America's war on drugs."
29. Eli Stokols, "Trump campaigns on border wall progress. There's not much of it," *Los Angeles Times*, June 23, 2020.
30. Quoted in Jeremy Berke, "Jeff Sessions says he will enforce federal law in an 'appropriate way'—and the marijuana industry is rattled," *Business Insider*, March 9, 2017.
31. Bruce M. Bagley and Jonathan D. Rosen, "The Trump Administration's Drug Policies: Subnational Trends and Challenges," *Internacionales. Revista en Ciencias Sociales del Pacífico Mexicano* Vol. 3 No. 6 (2018): pp. 38–61.
32. Quoted in Matt Ford, "Jeff Sessions Reinvigorates the Drug War," *The Atlantic*, May 12, 2017; Department of Justice (DOJ), Justice Department Issues Memo on Marijuana Enforcement, *DOJ*, https://www.justice.gov/opa/pr/justice-department-issues-memo-marijuana-enforcement, January 4, 2018, accessed June 29, 2020.
33. Quoted in Samuel Oakford, "Trump Gets 100 Countries to Sign on to his U.N. Drug War Plan, Ignoring Changing Thinking on Human Rights and Legalization," *The Intercept*, September 25, 2018.
34. Bruce M. Bagley and Jonathan D. Rosen, eds., *Drug Trafficking, Organized Crime, and Violence in the Americas Today* (Gainesville, FL: University Press of Florida, 2015): Roberto Zepeda and Jonathan D. Rosen, eds., *Cooperation and Drug Policies in the Americas: Trends in the Twenty-First* Century (Lanham, MD: Lexington Books, December 2014); Jonathan D. Rosen, *The Losing War: Plan Colombia and Beyond* (Albany, NY: State University of New York Press, 2014); Jonathan D. Rosen and Roberto Zepeda, *Organized Crime, Drug Trafficking, and Violence in Mexico: The Transition from Felipe Calderón to Enrique Peña Nieto* (Lanham, MD: Lexington Books, 2016).

35. For some excellent works, see: Christopher P. Krebs, Michael Costelloe, and David Jenks, "Drug control policy and smuggling innovation: a game-theoretic analysis," *Journal of Drug Issues* 33, no. 1 (2003): pp. 133–160; Benjamin Lessing, "Logics of violence in criminal war," *Journal of Conflict Resolution* 59, no. 8 (2015): 1486–1516; Christy A. Visher, Sara A. Debus-Sherrill, and Jennifer Yahner. "Employment after prison: A longitudinal study of former prisoners," *Justice Quarterly* 28, no. 5 (2011): pp. 698–718; Javier Osorio, "The contagion of drug violence: spatiotemporal dynamics of the Mexican war on drugs," *Journal of Conflict Resolution* 59, no. 8 (2015): pp. 1403–1432; Javier Osorio and Alejandro Reyes, "Supervised event coding from text written in Spanish: Introducing eventus id," *Social Science Computer Review* 35, no. 3 (2017): pp. 406–416.

36. José Miguel Cruz, Jonathan D. Rosen, Luis Enrique Amaya, and Yulia Vorobyeva, *The New Face of Street Gangs: The Gang Phenomenon in El Salvador* (Miami, FL: FIU, 2017); Jonathan D. Rosen and José Miguel Cruz, "Rethinking the Mechanisms of Gang Desistance in a Developing Country," *Deviant Behavior* (2018): pp. 1–15; Bruce M. Bagley and Jonathan D. Rosen, "The Trump Administration's Drug Policies: Subnational Trends and Challenges," *Internacionales. Revista en Ciencias Sociales del Pacífico Mexicano* Vol. 3 No. 6 (2018): 38–61; Jonathan D. Rosen y Roberto Zepeda Martínez, "La Guerra contra las Drogas y la Cooperación internacional: el caso de Colombia," *Revista CS*, No. 18 (2016): 63–84; Jonathan Daniel Rosen and Roberto Zepeda Martínez, "La guerra contra las drogas en Colombia y México: estrategias fracasadas," *Ánfora*, Vol. 21, No. 38 (2014): 179–200.

37. For more, see: Paul Gootenberg, *Andean Cocaine: The Making of a Global Drug* (Chapel Hill, NC: University of North Carolina Press, 2008); Edmundo Morales, "Coca and cocaine economy and social change in the Andes of Peru," *Economic Development and Cultural Change* 35, no. 1 (1986): pp. 143–161; Peter R. Andreas and Kenneth E. Sharpe, "Cocaine politics in the Andes," *Current History* 91, no. 562 (1992): p. 74.

38. Kate Doyle, "The militarization of the drug war in Mexico," *Current History* 92, no. 571 (1993): p. 83; Coletta Youngers, "Cocaine Madness Counternarcotics and Militarization in the Andes," *NACLA Report on the Americas* 34, no. 3 (2000): pp. 16–23.

39. Bruce Bagley, *Drug Trafficking and Organized Crime in the Americas: Major Trends in the Twenty-Frist Century* (Washington, DC: Woodrow Wilson Center International Center for Scholars, 2012).

40. Dina Perrone and Travis C. Pratt, "Comparing the quality of confinement and cost-effectiveness of public versus private prisons: What we know, why we do not know more, and where to go from here," *The Prison Journal* 83, no. 3 (2003): pp. 301–322; Travis C. Pratt and Jeff Maahs, "Are private prisons more cost-effective than public prisons? A meta-analysis of evaluation research studies," *Crime & Delinquency* 45, no. 3 (1999): pp. 358–371.

CHAPTER 2

The Drug War in Colombia

Abstract This chapter focuses on the war on drugs in Colombia. It begins by examining the linkages between cocaine trafficking between Colombia and South Florida, which elevated the drug trade on the security agenda of the United States. This chapter then examines the Medellín and Cali cartels and their role in drug trafficking and organized crime. It also analyzes Plan Colombia, a multi-billion-dollar foreign aid package designed to combat drug production and trafficking. This chapter explores how the goals of Plan Colombia evolved over time and the consequences of this policy. The chapter focuses on recent trends in coca production and the evolution of criminal groups, such as the criminal bands. Finally, it examines the impact of the peace process and the return to the war on drugs during the Duque administration.

Keywords Medellín cartel • Cali cartel • Plan Colombia • Miami • Pablo Escobar • Álvaro Uribe

Pablo Escobar, the notorious kingpin of one of the most profitable drug cartels that the world has ever seen, once stated: "All empires are created of blood and fire."[1] This chapter examines the evolution of drug trafficking and organized crime in Colombia. It starts with the Miami-Colombia connection and the role of the Medellín cartel. The Colombian government, with support of the United States, focused on toppling the major cartels. This chapter examines the role of counternarcotic programs, such as Plan Colombia. It focuses on the Uribe, Santos, and Duque administrations and the impact of the security strategies these three presidents had on organized crime. The Duque administration received pressure from Washington and is returning to hardline policies to combat the cultivation of coca, drug trafficking, and organized crime.

THE MIAMI-COLOMBIA CONNECTION

During the 1970s and 1980s, Griselda Blanco operated as one of the most powerful drug traffickers moving cocaine from Colombia to Miami. She became known as the Godmother (*La Madrina*) and the Black Widow, as it is alleged that she killed former lovers and husbands. She grew up in Medellín Colombia. Blanco came to the United States at the age of 17 and later became involved in the drug trade in Queens, New York.[2] She moved from New York to Miami and contributed to the "cocaine cowboy" reputation that characterized the city in the 1980s. Blanco dominated a drug enterprise that trafficked an estimated 3400 pounds of cocaine per month via aircraft and boats.[3] She conducted her operations in Miami and Fort Lauderdale, Florida, as well as New York. She also "pioneered" the concept of drug mules, women who transported marijuana and cocaine. She worked with the leaders of the Medellín cartel, who took advantage of the drug trafficking networks that she established.[4] Blanco operated her drug network with three of her sons with a penchant for violence and scoring revenges of people who crossed her or her drug trafficking enterprise. Blanco is known for indiscriminate violence used to send messages to rival criminal organizations.[5]

In 1979, for instance, authorities linked her to the massive shooting at Dadeland Mall, a well-known destination in Miami for shopping for locals as well as tourists. Authorities, however, could only convict her on three murders, including her involvement in the murder of a two-year-old named Johnny Castro, the son of Jesus "Chucho." Jorge Ayala, a hitman for Blanco, indicated that the Godmother wanted Chucho killed because he had kicked her son, which she named Michael Corleone Blanco. Johnny Castro died from gunshot wounds while in the backseat of the car. Castro's father survived, which originally angered Blanco. According to Ayala, "At first she was real mad 'cause we missed the father." He continued, "But when she heard we had gotten the son by accident, she said she was glad, that they were even."⁶ This case shows the ruthless nature of Blanco, who did not hesitate to kill innocent children.

Blanco went to prison for two decades for three murders, including the killing of Johnny Castro. U.S. authorities deported her back to Colombia in 2004, and gunmen riding on a motorcycle shot her in Medellín. Ironically, Blanco invented the "motorcycle assassin," which is when gunmen ride by the human targets and shoot them. Some authorities expressed levels of surprise that she had not been murdered earlier in her criminal career, given her long list of enemies. Nelson Andreu, a former homicide detective in Miami, stated: "It's surprising to all of us that she had not been killed sooner because she made a lot of enemies. He continued, "When you kill so many and hurt so many people like she did, it's only a matter of time before they find you and try to even the score."⁷

The cocaine cowboy era in Miami included a wide array of characters, including John Roberts, known as "the bearded gringo." Authorities in the United States called him the "American Representative" of the Medellín cartel for his role in the cocaine trade. Roberts, a New York native, moved to Miami in 1975 after one of his business associates died; one police informant said that John Roberts had been involved in this crime. According to Roberts, "When I first came to Miami, I wasn't smuggling: I was like all the other dealers on the street just trying to make a living, and it got to a point where I had so much business that these people just couldn't supply me."⁸ Roberts became involved further in the criminal underworld becoming a major drug importer for the Medellín cartel, which will be analyzed in the sections below. According to Roberts, he "moved" $500,000 or more of cocaine each month from Colombia to South Florida. Roberts and his associates developed different mechanisms for importing cocaine into South Florida, including the utilization of secret airfields. This cast of characters would fly aircraft several hours north of Miami to avoid suspicion of authorities looking to stop planes coming from South America. They would then load a car onto a tow-truck and drive the cocaine-loaded car from Tampa to Florida.⁹ This criminal network also would listen to U.S. authorities on the radio and attempt to avoid detection. Authorities captured Roberts in 1992 after he evaded law enforcement for five years. Facing the pressure from federal authorities, Roberts cooperated with the government, which enabled him to serve a reduced prison sentence. He left prison in 2000 and returned to South Florida until his death from cancer in 2011.¹⁰

The Medellín and Cali Cartels

Colombia had two major cartels that dominated drug trafficking during the 1980s and early 1990s: the Medellín and Cali cartels.[11] Pablo Escobar, the leader of the Medellín cartel, utilized indiscriminate violence to dominate the cocaine industry—at one point the cartel supplied 80 percent of the world's cocaine. The lucrative cocaine industry made Escobar extremely wealthy. In fact, sources indicate that Escobar had become the seventh richest individual in the world in 1989, demonstrating the massive fortune that he acquired through his drug trafficking empire.[12]

The Medellín cartel had a cast of characters, including, Carlos Lehder, known as "Crazy Charlie" for his erratic behavior. Lehder became a very useful asset for the Medellín cartel as he revolutionized the way that the cartel moved drugs.[13] Ledher grew up in Colombia and moved to the United States in the 1960s. While in the United States, he participated in small-scale crime, including selling marijuana, which led to him being removed from the country. While in Colombia, Lehder implemented the utilization of small aircraft to move cocaine, which enabled the quantity of drugs shipped to be expanded exponentially compared to the previous methods of drug mules transporting narcotics on commercial airlines. He even purchased an island in the Bahamas that the cartel utilized as a strategic location for transporting drugs to the United States. Escobar tolerated Ledher, whose utility to the cartel declined over time. In fact, Ron Chepesiuk, the author of a book on Ledher titled *Crazy Charlie: Revolutionary or Neo-Nazi* maintains, "With time, as Lehder's value decreased to the cartel and he became what the Medellin Cartel considered a public embarrassment and even a liability, Escobar reached the point where he did not respect Lehder. Frankly, I'm surprised that Escobar didn't have Carlos killed."[14] Rumors even emerged that Escobar provided information that eventually led to Ledher's extradition to the United States. In 1988, a judge sentenced Ledher to 135 years, but four years later his sentence decreased to 55 years after he agreed to testify against the Panamanian dictator, Manuel Noriega.[15]

The Medellín cartel under Escobar's leadership used its money and power to expand and penetrate the state apparatus in Colombia. Escobar used his money and power to bribe police officers, judges, and government officials. The saying *Plata o Plomo*, which is Spanish for silver or lead, best describes the negotiating system utilized by Escobar, who was infamous for his violent tactics. Escobar would offer police officers a bribe (i.e., the *plata*), or they would face the consequences. The Medellín kingpin did not survive by making empty promises, but rather he instilled fear into police officers and judges.[16]

Escobar's greed continued and he even became an elected official, serving as an alternate in the Colombian Congress. His son, Sebastián Marroquín, maintains that this political power maneuver constituted his father's biggest mistake.[17] Prior to this point, the political and socioeconomic elite tolerated Escobar. The Medellín kingpin "overstepped an invisible boundary"[18] when he started to get involved in politics. Public officials viewed it as an outrage that a known drug trafficker became involved in the Colombian Congress. The Justice Minister, Rodrigo Lara Bonilla, denounced Pablo Escobar and had him investigated and removed from Congress. *El Espectador* newspaper published works about Escobar, and the Medellín cartel boss had the journalist who published the story killed.[19] A car and two gunmen on a motorcycle also killed Bonilla, a crusader for justice and combating corruption, in May 1984 in northern Bogotá.[20]

Escobar increased the violent attacks not only against police officers and judges but also against presidential candidates. In 1989, Escobar had presidential candidate Luis Carlos Galan murdered during a campaign rally. President Virgilio Barco Vargas responded to the increasing levels of violence by reinstating the extradition treaty, which the newly minted 1991 Constitution had prohibited. The Medellín cartel leader feared being extradited to the United States, declaring that he would rather die in a grave in Colombia than sit in a prison in the United States.[21] It would have been much more difficult for Escobar to operate his Medellín cartel enterprise from a maximum security prison or the supermax security prison in Florence, Colorado, which opened in November 1994 and houses some of the most violent and dangerous criminals in the United States.[22]

The Medellín drug capo forced the Colombian government to the negotiating table after kidnapping seemingly countless citizens, including the daughter of a former Colombian president.[23] To avoid extradition, Escobar negotiated his own incarceration. The Colombian government believed that having Escobar incarcerated could help them at least know where he was and control his activities. Yet Escobar's prison did not resemble a penitentiary as it had game rooms, a soccer field, and even a waterfall. Escobar hand-selected the "prison" guards, who provided the drug kingpin with significant latitude. The drug boss ran his multi-billion-dollar enterprise while in his spacious prison, but he took breaks to host wild prison parties. His parties included drugs, alcohol, and prostitutes. It is also rumored that Escobar played soccer with the skull of the victim functioning as the soccer ball.[24]

The situation in the prison became unruly—even for Escobar's standards—as the Medellín capo murdered people while incarcerated, forcing the government to attempt to transfer him to another facility. Escobar escaped from prison after being "incarcerated" for just over 400 days,[25] and the Colombian government, with the assistance of the U.S. government, began a nationwide search for Escobar.[26]

The Colombian authorities, with support from the Drug Enforcement Administration (DEA), located Escobar when he made a call to his son in 1993. The Colombian police killed Escobar, who was hiding out in Medellín. There, however, has been some controversy over whether the police killed Escobar or whether he committed suicide. In his book, *Pablo Escobar: My Father*, Sebastián Marroquín maintains that his father committed suicide. Yet this claim has been denied by many authorities, including Stephen Murphy, the DEA agent who helped capture Escobar.[27]

The Cali cartel increased in power after the demise of the Medellín cartel. By 1994, some experts referred to the Cali cartel as the "kings of cocaine."[28] The Colombian government eventually toppled the Cali cartel. The collapse of the Medellín and Cali cartel resulted in a fragmentation of organized crime as hundreds of small cartels emerged to fill the vacuum left by the demise of these large criminal organizations. Yet while the demise of Escobar represented a victory for Colombia, it did not lead to the termination of drug trafficking and organized crime.[29] Criminal actors are opportunists and will respond to government strategy and the changing landscape of the criminal cartels. The demise of a major organization represents an opportunity for other criminal actors looking to become more involved in drug trafficking and increase their revenue streams.

Plan Colombia and Beyond: Combating Drug Trafficking and Organized Crime

Andrés Pastrana served as the President of Colombia from 1998 to 2002 and sought to bring peace to Colombia. President Pastrana desired to negotiate with the FARC, the largest guerilla organization in the country, to decrease crime and violence. He wanted to gain the trust of the FARC and granted them a demilitarized zone where the police and military would not enter. This plan backfired as the FARC relocated combatants into this zone and coordinated their criminal operations from this area, which was the size of Switzerland.[30]

As the Colombian economic and security situation began to spiral downward, President Pastrana sought assistance from the U.S. government. President Pastrana wanted the United States and international community to fund a plan to help Colombia achieve peace and end its decades-long internal armed conflict. Pastrana believed that Colombia could not address drug trafficking and organized crime without solving the internal conflict. The United States, however, did not want to become immersed in the armed conflict of a foreign country and altered the initiative proposed by President Pastrana. General Barry McCaffrey, the head of the Office of National Drug Control Policy (ONDCP), played a crucial part in the reorientation of Plan Colombia and the role of the United States in the initiative.[31] The Clinton administration expressed concern over drug trafficking and organized crime in Colombia. President Clinton signed Plan Colombia in to law in 2000 after the U.S. Congress passed the initiative. The new plan allocated 80 percent of the resources to help strengthen the military and police and decrease coca cultivation through the spraying of herbicides from aircraft. Critics maintain that Plan Colombia focused on the drug supply and could best be described as a militarized plan. Yet the focus on the supply of drugs failed to solve the underlying issues such as the demand for drugs as well as the high levels of corruption and institutional weakness in Colombia.[32]

Plan Colombia evolved over time. President Bush assumed office and changed foreign policy priorities after the events of September 11, 2001. As a presidential candidate, many individuals criticized Bush for his limited foreign policy experience. For instance, he could not name the leader of Pakistan, referring to Pervez Musharraf as the general. Candidate Bush also told critics that he had a close relationship with the leadership of Mexico while governor of Texas. Yet the terrorist attacks on September 11 changed the foreign policy goals of the Bush administration as it launched a global war on terrorism. The Bush administration prioritized foreign policy and national security over domestic politics.

President Uribe recognized that he had to change the perceptions of the Colombian conflict to meet the national security goals of the United States. Uribe contended that Colombia did not have an internal armed conflict between various armed actors. Instead, he maintained that this

South American country had narco-terrorists. The Bush administration bought into the reorientation of Plan Colombia. Plan Colombia also provided the Bush government an opportunity to respond to critics who contended that the global war on terror focused only on the Middle East. The Bush administration pointed to Colombia, the oldest democracy in the Americas, and maintained that the U.S. government would respond to terrorism around the globe.

President Bush changed the discourse about the Colombian conflict and vowed to support his ally, President Uribe, in the fight against terrorism. During a meeting at the Casa de Nariño in Bogotá in March 2007, President Bush emphasized his commitment to support this South American ally through Plan Colombia, stating:

> I'm looking forward very much to talking and continuing to work with you to defeat the drug lords and narco-traffickers -- narco-terrorists. You recognize, like I recognize, that the most important function of state is to provide security for its people. You cannot tolerate in a society the ability of people to take innocent life to achieve political objectives. And so I appreciate your steadfast strength, and so do the people of this country.
>
> I am looking forward to working with you on the second phase -- or the next phase of Plan Colombia. We're going to work with your government to continue to fight drug trafficking. The United States has an obligation to work to reduce the demand for drugs, and at the same time, work to interdict the supply of drugs. There's a lot we can do. But part of it is to help you exercise control over all your territory; is to strengthen the rule of law, and to expand economic opportunity for the citizens. And we want to help.[33]

The Bush administration not only vowed to support its South American ally in terms of the new security-driven rhetoric, but the U.S. government increased foreign aid to Colombia. Funding spiked from $276.2 million in FY 2001 to $562.2 million in FY 2002. The aid continued to increase during the Bush government. In FY 2005, for instance, Colombia received $813.8 million from the U.S. government. Most of the resources went to funding the military and counternarcotic programs as opposed to focusing on institutional strengthening and addressing underlying structural issues (e.g., impunity, corruption, and lack of transparency) (Fig. 2.1).

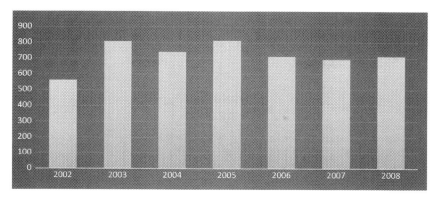

Fig. 2.1 United States funding for plan Colombia (in millions of dollars). (Source: Created by author with data from June S. Beittel and Claire Ribando Seelke, *Colombia: Issues for Congress* (Washington, DC: Congressional Research Service, 2009); State Department Foreign Operations Congressional Budget Justifications; FY2006 Foreign Operations Appropriations Act, P.L. 109–102, and conference report, H.Rept. 109–265)

COCA, COCAINE, AND ORGANIZED CRIME

The Colombian government sought to combat coca cultivation because it is a major source of revenue for organized crime groups. President Uribe argued that the state needed to decrease the ability of these criminal groups to earn money from the lucrative cocaine trade. One of the most controversial initiatives designed to combat the cultivation of coca is aerial spraying. Coca cultivation, however, is not an urban phenomenon but a rural problem that occurs in areas of the country that are vastly ungoverned by the state.[34]

The spraying of herbicides from aircraft has been criticized by many experts. Pilots can miss the targets because of external factors, such as wind, which is referred to as spray drift.[35] Farmers who make their living cultivating coca also have adjusted to the use of aircraft to spray herbicides by planting coca along with licit crops, making it much more difficult to identify coca from satellites. Missing targets can cause serious environmental damages, ruining licit crops and impacting biodiversity in rural

Colombia. Finally, aerial spraying can cause serious health issues for people living in these regions.[36]

Many experts have contended that aerial eradication programs are counterproductive. While coca production can decline in certain regions in the short term, it merely shifts to other departments within Colombia or even neighboring countries—this is an example of the balloon effect. Adam Isacson of the Washington Office on Latin America (WOLA) argues that "[t]he experience in Colombia between the early 1990s and the mid-2010s showed that fumigation could achieve short-term reductions in coca cultivation in specific areas. In the medium and long term, though, crops recovered as growers adjusted. They did so through replanting, growing more plants to minimize lost harvests, cutting back plants to save them immediately after spraying, and other strategies."[37] Thus, coca cultivation in the long term is not only ineffective, but it has serious health and environmental hazards.

Scholars also maintain that decreasing coca cultivation by aerial fumigation programs and crop substitution have not been effective because small-scale farmers in Colombia continue to grow coca because it is more profitable than cultivating other crops. Coca grows in the Andes Mountains and jungle, which is not the same for other crops, such as oranges. Marten W. Brienen, an expert on drug trafficking and organized crime, argues that coca grows everywhere, which is not true for other crops.[38] He maintains that the only way to destroy coca is to light it on fire. Brienen notes that there are major infrastructure challenges as transporting goods, such as oranges—even if they did grow in the Colombian jungle—would require *campesinos* to traverse rural parts of Colombia that lack paved roads. This could require days, which would cause the goods to spoil good by the time they reach the market. Peasant farmers also receive more money for cultivating coca than growing coffee or oranges. Finally, there is a security dilemma as farmers could be threatened by criminal actors if they do not cultivate coca.

SECURITY IMPROVES BUT COCA CULTIVATION AND DRUG TRAFFICKING CONTINUE

The Uribe administration had some successes in terms of improving security metrics. For instance, the homicide rate decreased from more than 28,000 in 2002 to 17,479 in 2006. By 2010, Colombia had 15,459

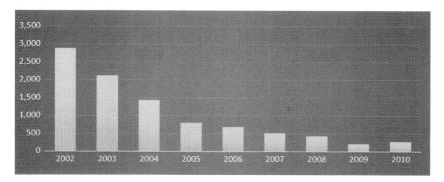

Fig. 2.2 Kidnappings in Colombia during the Uribe administration. (Source: Created by author with data from Washington Office on Latin America, 15th *Anniversary of Plan Colombia: Learning from Its Successes and Failures* (Washington, DC: WOLA, 2016); Ministry of Defense of Colombia)

homicides, representing a significant improvement. Moreover, the number of massacre victims dropped from 680 in 2002 to 193 in 2006. By 2009, Colombia had 147 massacre victims. Kidnappings declined significantly from more than 2800 in 2002 to 1440 in 2004. By 2009, Colombia recorded 213 kidnappings. While Colombia witnessed declines in the number of forced displacements, they have remained quite high (Fig. 2.2).

While Plan Colombia had some successes with the capturing of leaders of various criminal organizations, drug trafficking and organized crime continued unabated as there is always another leader waiting in line to take over the highly lucrative, albeit dangerous, drug trafficking industry. As history reveals, capturing one kingpin often results in the fragmentation of organized crime, and it can cause infighting within and between organizations for power, routes, and territory. It, therefore, is a mistake to assume that drug trafficking organizations are static and do not evolve overtime. Some organizations implode, while other organizations increase in power.

Drug traffickers have less loyalty than gangs, which revolve around identity—so much so that gangs like MS-13 often tattoo gang symbols on their bodies. On the other hand, drug traffickers are loyal to one thing: money. They are willing to switch organizations if the money is right. A sports analogy would be that just as NBA players change teams and uniforms for the organization that will pay them the most or give them the best chance of winning, there have been documented cases of traffickers switching criminal organizations.

Despite Plan Colombia's efforts to combat drug production and trafficking, coca cultivation has remained steady over the years, only declining drastically between 2008 and 2009. In December 2004, the United Nations Office on Drugs and Crime (UNODC) reported that Colombia cultivated more than 80,000 hectares of coca. In December 2005, the total hectares of coca under cultivation increased to more than 85,000 but declined to 77,870 hectares in December 2006. Yet in December 2007, coca cultivation spiked to 98,899 hectares. While the Uribe administration saw a decline in coca cultivation in December 2009 to just over 68,000 hectares, some departments within Colombia experienced increases in cultivation. Guaviare, Cauca, and Córdoba saw 26, 13, and 63 percent increases, respectively, between 2008 and 2009.[39]

CRIMINAL BANDS, DRUG TRAFFICKING, AND HUMAN RIGHTS ABUSES

While the Uribe administration experienced security improvements, critics highlight the major human rights abuses that occurred during this time period.[40] President Uribe had close connections between the right wing-paramilitaries known as the United Self-Defense Forces of Colombia (Autodefensas Unidas de Colombia—AUC). While the Uribe administration denied linkages to the paramilitary actors, investigative reports indicate that nearly half of the Colombian Congress had connections to the paramilitaries. Reports even emerged about Uribe's family members having linkages to the paramilitary forces. Investigations have revealed that paramilitaries operated out of a ranch owned by the former president. Santiago Uribe, the brother of the former president, had intricate connections to an organization known as the Twelve Apostles, a group that operated as a death squad throughout the Colombian countryside and killed supporters of the left-wing guerilla organization. One former Colombian police official, Juan Carlos Meneses Quintero, indicated that this death squad trained at the Uribe's ranch, indicating the close connections that the paramilitaries had with the Uribe family clan. Meneses has argued that the death squads performed "social cleansing" by efforts to "assassinate petty criminals, drug addicts, and guerrilla supporters."[41] These intricate linkages between the Uribe family and the paramilitaries became harder for the former president to deny, even though he claimed that such accounts constituted tails invented by his political opponents and enemies.

In addition to the paramilitary scandals, President Uribe faced security challenges in terms of drug trafficking and organized crime, which continued unabated. The number of criminal actors also started to increase. President Uribe praised the demobilization of more than 32,000 members of the AUC as a major victory for Colombia. Some law enforcement officials maintain that the criminal bands are a result of the success of law enforcement activities against major Colombian drug trafficking networks. Mark R. Trouville of the DEA, for example, argues: "Law enforcement's success in removing the leadership of the major Colombian drug trafficking organizations has resulted in smaller groups, or bands of criminals, coming together to continue large scale importation of cocaine into the United States."[42] Yet critics maintain that the criminal landscape in Colombia has shifted as these organizations have morphed into drug trafficking groups and various criminal bands, often referred to as the BACRIM.

The Rastrojos emerged in 2002 from the Norte de Valle drug trafficking organization and became a major player in the Colombian criminal underworld. This organization served as a military unit for Wilber Varela who was at war with a rival within the Norte de Valle Cartel, Diego Montoya, or "Don Diego." The organization began to expand throughout Colombia, operating in more than a third of the country's territory. The Rostrojos became one of the most powerful criminal bands in Colombia by 2010, but the group later suffered major defeats and imploded after the capture of the key leaders of this powerful criminal organization.[43] In 2011, a federal court in Brooklyn charged ten leaders of the Rastrojos. The court charged Javier Antonio Calle Serna, known by his alias "Comba," with murder and for operating a "continuing criminal enterprise." The indictment indicates that the federal government would seek the forfeiture of assets totaling around a billion dollars gained from criminal activities.[44] Calle Serna later turned himself into the U.S. government, while authorities captured two other leaders, including Diego Rastrojo, and extradited them to the United States. U.S. Attorney Wifredo A. Ferrer, contended: "The Southern District of Florida is the first and best line of defense against the importation of mass quantities of cocaine into our borders." He vowed that the U.S. government will continue to combat the BACRIM and their criminal endeavors. He maintained, "The United States government will not rest until we eradicate the BACRIMs and destroy their ability to ply their trade, as we did the former drug cartels."[45] Other experts, such as Marc Chernick, however, have a more critical perspective and defined the demobilization as a farce as the AUC did not really demobilize,[46] but rather they fragmented into other criminal actors that are involved in drug trafficking and organized crime.

The Urabeños also emerged out of the demobilization of the AUC and are one of the most powerful criminal groups in Colombia today. The Urabeños are led by Dairo Antonio Úsuga David.[47] This criminal group operates in 13 Colombian departments and is involved in drug trafficking and the processing of cocaine. The Southern District of New York indicted Usuga David in 2009, and the U.S. Department of State has offered up to $5 million for information leading to the arrest or conviction of this individual.[48]

The Santos Administration: Peace, Demobilization, and Drug Trafficking

Juan Manuel Santos assumed the presidency in 2010. Previously, Santos served as head of the Ministry of Defense, where he was responsible for overseeing military operations, including the campaigns against the FARC as well as the military's involvement in counternarcotics operations. President Santos angered Uribe to no avail when he announced publicly that the Colombian government would participate in peace negotiations with the FARC, following two years of secret negotiations between 2010 and 2012. The peace accord lasted for four years and occurred in Havana, Cuba.

In September 2016, the Colombian government made history and signed a peace accord with the FARC. The Santos government asked Colombians to vote if they supported the peace deal in a plebiscite. Colombians expressed their concerns and disapproval of the controversial peace agreement with the largest guerilla organization as the no vote won in the plebiscite. The Santos government revised the peace accord. The Colombian Congress approved a new version of the peace accord in November 2016, and President Santos won the Nobel Peace Prize for his efforts to bring an end to the more than 50-year internal armed conflict.[49]

While the peace accord passed, it cost Santos politically as his popularity declined over time as the FARC is a highly distrusted organization. According to the Latin American Public Opinion Project (LAPOP) 2018/2019 survey conducted by Vanderbilt University, only 1.12 percent of Colombians responded that they have "a lot" of trust in the FARC, while 61.90 percent responded "none." Many Colombians have a long memory of the many violent acts that the FARC have been involved in, and society does not trust that the FARC will stop partaking in criminal activities. According to the 2016/2017 LAPOP data, for example, 41.42 percent of Colombians answered "very unlikely" when asked about the likelihood that the FARC will stop trafficking drugs after the peace accord, while 41.62 percent answered "unlikely." The survey also indicates that 40.98 percent of Colombians said no when asked about whether they agree with the reintegration of the FARC. Moreover, 48.34 percent of the population answered no when asked if forgiveness and reconciliation are possible between Colombians citizens and the FARC. Finally, 27.37 percent of the population stated "very unlikely" when asked the likelihood that the FARC demobilizes after the peace agreement, while 40.18 answered "unlikely" (Fig. 2.3).

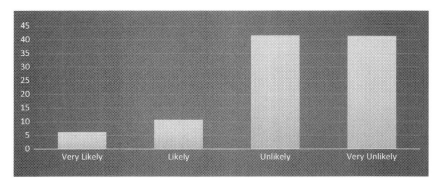

Fig. 2.3 Colombian's perceptions about the likelihood of the FARC stopping drug trafficking after a peace agreement. (Source: Created by author with LAPOP 2016/2017 data)

The demobilization of the FARC presents a variety of security obstacles.[50] The reintegration of the FARC requires that Colombian society provide former combatants with opportunities. Many of the FARC soldiers are from some of the most marginalized zones within the country and lack education and the necessary job skills to compete in today's globalized world. Reintegrating former FARC soldiers requires investing resources in this process. It also requires that Colombian society provide job opportunities for former FARC soldiers. Guerrilla fighters who have committed criminal acts who are unable to find employment in the licit economy could return to what they know: the criminal underworld. The FARC are joining other criminal organizations, causing some experts to label them as the FARCRIM.[51] These FARC dissidents are participating in a variety of illicit activities and have contributed to violence in different regions within Colombia, such as Nariño. The FARC dissidents not only are fighting for control of drug trafficking but also with other groups such as the Urabeños.

While the Santos administration's peace accord with the FARC represented a historic moment despite the many challenges reinserting FARC soldiers back into society, Colombia has continued to face obstacles regarding drug trafficking and organized crime. In 2015, President Santos suspended aerial fumigation programs after the findings of the World Health Organization, which indicated that glyphosate, the major ingredient used to spray coca, could cause cancer. The result is that coca cultivation spiked: it increased from 96,084 hectares in December 2015 to 171,495 in December 2017 (Fig. 2.4).

The increase in coca cultivation also resulted in cocaine production skyrocketing. The export quality of Colombian cocaine increased from 270 metric tons in 2012 to 690 metric tons in 2015. By 2016, Colombia had a total export quality of 910 metric tons of cocaine. Moreover, the purity of cocaine has remained relatively stable, and it has increased in recent years. In 2007, for instance, cocaine exported from Colombia had a 61.1 percent purity. This number declined to 45.90 percent in 2010. In 2015, Colombian cocaine had a 49 percent purity, but the levels increased to 56.40 percent in 2016.[52]

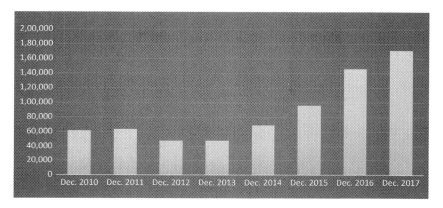

Fig. 2.4 Coca cultivation in Colombia (in hectares). (Source: Created by author with data from United Nations Office on Drugs and Crime (UNODC), *Colombia: Monitoreo de territorios afectados por cultivos ilícitos 2017* (Bogotá, CO: Colombia, 2018))

THE ELECTION OF DUQUE AND THE RETURN TO THE WAR ON DRUGS

Iván Duque ran for president with the support of Álvaro Uribe. Many Colombians had never heard of Duque prior to his presidential run. Candidate Duque represented a rejection of President Santos' policies, particularly negotiating with the FARC. Duque tapped into Colombians distrust and resentment of the FARC and fear that insecurity in the country was increasing. According to the 2016/2017 LAPOP data, for instance, 25.10 percent of Colombians responded that they had been a victim of a crime in the last 12 months. Of the people who responded that they had been a victim, 54.85 percent contended that they had been a victim once, 24.23 responded twice, and 10.20 percent said three times.

Colombia has received pressure from the United States to combat coca cultivation, drug production, and trafficking. While President Trump praised Duque as a nice guy, he criticized the new president for not helping the United States combat drug trafficking in Colombia. In March 2019, Trump stated: "I'll tell you something: Colombia, you have your new president of Colombia, really good guy. I've met him, we had him at the White House. He said how he was going to stop drugs. More drugs are coming out of Colombia right now than before he was president—so he has done nothing for us."[53] These remarks demonstrated President Trump's concern over the production of coca and increased the pressure on the Colombian president.

Yet critics maintained that the U.S. government needs to redefine the issue of success. Simply meeting the targets of coca sprayed by herbicides does not signify that the United States is "winning" the war on drugs. Jeremy McDermott echoes this point, stating: "Until now, the main measures of 'success' in the drug war have been reducing the number of hectares of coca under cultivation, cocaine seizures and the extradition of top drug traffickers. This is all well and good, but these strategies only deal with a fraction of the links in the drug chain. And the obsession with these measurables has placed Colombia on what former president Juan Manuel Santos described as an exercise bicycle, where pedaling furiously gets you nowhere."[54] Focusing only on combating the supply of drugs does not solve the underlying structural issues that foster drug trafficking and organized crime in Colombia (e.g., poverty, inequality, impunity, and corruption). And simply combating the supply of drugs does not address the issue of demand. Drug trafficking will continue if the demand for these products exist.

President Duque has vowed to ramp up the war on drugs. One of the most controversial measures has been the debate over aerial spraying. President Trump continued to pressure Duque over time to return to aerial spraying. During a March 2020 meeting at the White House with President Duque, Trump contended: "You're going to have to spray." He continued, "If you don't spray you're not going to get rid of (the coca), so you have to spray with regard to the drugs in Colombia."[55] That same month, the Duque administration indicated that the country would restart aerial spraying to combat coca cultivation.

Returning to aerial spraying is troublesome as this policy has not worked and has had significant collateral damages. History shows that campesino farmers simply shift where they plant coca. They also plant the crop with other licit crops, making it more difficult for aircraft to detect coca from the sky. In addition, the health and environmental consequences of spraying herbicides are well documented, leading critics to argue that not only is aerial spraying ineffective, but it is counterproductive. Isacson echoes this point, stating: "What both countries are ignoring is the lack of evidence supporting aerial fumigation as an effective long-term drug control strategy. The plan also ignores the very real possibility that restarting fumigation will result in grave consequences for communities in vulnerable situations."[56] The Duque administration, facing pressure from its neighbor to the north, is ramping up the war on drugs despite the collateral damages of policies such as aerial spraying.

The Duque government began aerial eradication during the Covid-19 pandemic. In April 2020, security forces injured three people and killed one person protesting police efforts to eradicate coca in the Awa indigenous community located in Southwest Colombia. This death set an alarming precedent as it constituted the second death involving the manual eradication of coca since the Colombian government announced a quarantine in March 2020. Manual eradication, as the name implies, is the manual removal of coca from the ground.[57] History reveals that this process is ineffective as farmers can replant coca after the crops have been removed. There also are major security challenges as criminal organizations have placed landmines in coca fields. The Duque government is increasing eradication efforts as today there are around 150 "eradication teams," which is a drastic increase from the 25 that existed in 2017.[58] Human rights organizations have expressed concerns about citizen security and the steady wave of attacks against social leaders. Many of these killings of social leaders have gone unpunished, which send a lesson to FARC-dissident groups: they will not be punished for killing social leaders and activists.

The Duque government faces not only challenges with increasing coca cultivation but also the changing nature of organized crime. Drug traffickers have evolved and learned from the mistakes of past drug kingpins. Today, Colombia is witnessing arguably its fourth generation of drug traffickers known as "the invisibles." This new generation has recognized that flying under the radar is better for business than attracting large amounts of attention. This new generation does not carry guns or have cocaine on them, but rather they use technological innovations to take advantage of globalization. They launder money and hide their money through a diverse array of licit businesses, making it harder to trace the dirty money.[59] The increasing ability of the Colombian security intelligence services to identify and track drug traffickers has resulted in the new generation in the criminal underworld learning from the lessons of the past and becoming more sophisticated to avoid detection.

Combating organized crime requires what is a whole-of-government approach as one agency alone cannot solve the problem. The police, for instance, cannot arrest their way out of the problem. Intricately linked to this is the need for reforms across institutions. Colombia has major challenges with impunity as the impunity rate is over 90 percent. Reforming the police, as occurred during the Uribe administration, will not solve the problem if drug trafficking and organized crime groups can bribe judges and avoid prosecution. Unless these underlying issues are addressed, drug trafficking will continue to flourish.

Conclusion

Colombia has been at the center of the U.S.-led war on drugs for decades. While the Colombian government has seen the capture of drug kingpins, such as Pablo Escobar, and the demise of major criminal organizations, the drug trafficking and organized crime landscape has simply morphed into different criminal actors. Colombia faces an increasing number of actors as drug trafficking and organized crime have evolved over the past several decades. While the U.S. government invested $10 billion in Plan Colombia to help the Colombian government combat drug trafficking and organized crime, drug trafficking organizations have penetrated the state apparatus and have contributed to the high levels of corruption and impunity. Moreover, state fragility and corruption have enabled organized crime groups to thrive.[60]

While homicides have decreased and other security metrics have improved, drug trafficking and organized crime continue to flourish. Today, 90 percent of the cocaine coming to the United States is from Colombia. The Trump administration pressured the Colombian government to reduce the supply of cocaine, despite the countless scholarly and policy works discussing the failures of supply-side strategies. The Duque government is returning to aerial fumigation programs even though such policies are ineffective and have significant environmental and health consequences.

Notes

1. Michael W. Parra and José Mauricio Suárez-Becerra, "Twenty Years after the Killing of the King of Kingpins Pablo Escobar: Lessons Learned from Narco-Terrorism," *Journal Trauma Treatment* 1, no. 113 (2012): pp. 1–2.
2. Johnny Diaz, "Miami 'cocaine godmother' Griselda Blanco's story is a Lifetime TV movie with Catherine Zeta-Jones," *Sun Sentinel,* January 18, 2018; Alice Tregunna, "Cocaine cowgirl: the outrageous life and mysteri-

ous death of Griselda Blanco, the godmother of Medellin," *Trends in Organized Crime* 17, no. 1–2 (2014): pp. 132–134; Christopher M. White, *The War on Drugs in the Americas* (New York, NY: Routledge, 2019).
3. *The Miami Herald*, "Bullets once flew at Dadeland Mall in a deadly shootout. The Cocaine Cowboys were here," *The Miami Herald*, June 23, 2019; Directed by Billy Corben, "Cocaine Cowboys," Miami, Florida, Rakontur, 2006.
4. Arlene B. Tickner, Laura Alonso, Lara Loaiza, Natalia Suárez, Diana Castellanos, and Juan Diego Cárdenas, *Women and Organized Crime in Latin America: beyond victims or victimizers* (Bogotá, CO: El Observatorio Colombiano de Crimen Organizado and InSight Crime, 2020).
5. Arlene B. Tickner, Laura Alonso, Lara Loaiza, Natalia Suárez, Diana Castellanos, and Juan Diego Cárdenas, *Women and Organized Crime in Latin America: beyond victims or victimizers*.
6. Quoted in David Ovalle, "'Cocaine godmother' Griselda Blanco gunned down in Colombia," *The Miami Herald*, February 19, 2019.
7. Quoted in *The Miami Herald*, "Bullets once flew at Dadeland Mall in a deadly shootout. The Cocaine Cowboys were here."
8. NPR Staff, "From Mafia Soldier To Cocaine Cowboy," *NPR*, October 30, 2011.
9. See: Directed by Billy Corben, "Cocaine Cowboys."
10. NPR Staff, "From Mafia Soldier To Cocaine Cowboy," *NPR*, October 30, 2011; John Roberts and Evan Wright, *American Desperado: My Life--From Mafia Soldier to Cocaine Cowboy to Secret Government Asset* (New York, NY: Broadway Paperbacks, 2011).
11. For more, see: Bruce Michael Bagley, "Dateline drug wars: Colombia: the wrong strategy," *Foreign Policy* 77 (1989): pp. 154–171; Russell Crandall, *Driven by drugs: US policy toward Colombia* (Boulder, CO: Lynne Rienner Publishers, 2002); Russell Crandall, "Explicit narcotization: US policy toward Colombia during the Samper administration," *Latin American Politics and Society* 43, no. 3 (2001): pp. 95–120.
12. Amanda Macias, "10 facts reveal the absurdity of Pablo Escobar's wealth," *Business Insider*, September 21, 2015; Benjamin Lessing, *Making Peace in Drug Wars: Crackdowns and Cartels in Latin America* (New York, NY: Cambridge University Press, 2018); María Fernanda Lander, "La voz impenitente de la "sicaresca" colombiana," *Revista Iberoamericana* 73, no. 218 (2007): pp. 287–299; Adolfo León Atehortúa Cruz and Diana Marcela Rojas Rivera, "El narcotráfico en Colombia. Pioneros y capos," *Historia y espacio* 31 (2008): p. 7; Robert Filippone, "The Medellin Cartel: Why we can't win the drug war," *Studies in Conflict & Terrorism* 17, no. 4 (1994): pp. 323–344.

13. For more, see: Eduardo Saenz, "Between Carlos Lehder and the Cocaine Cowboys: The Consolidation of the Colombian Drug Dealing Networks in Miami in the 70s," *Cuadernos de Economía* 30, no. 54 (2011): p. 105; Andres Lopez Restrepo and Alvaro Camacho Guizado, "From smugglers to warlords: twentieth century colombian drug traffickers," *Canadian Journal of Latin American and Caribbean Studies* 28, no. 55–56 (2003): pp. 249–275; Bruce M. Bagley, "Colombia and the War on Drugs," *Foreign Affairs* 67, no. 1 (1988): pp. 70–92.
14. Quoted in Seth Ferranti, "The Nazi-Loving Drug Lord Who Revolutionized the Cocaine Smuggling Industry," *Vice*, January 9, 2016.
15. Associated Press, "Cocaine Smuggler Sentenced to Life," *The New York Times*, July 21, 1988; Seth Ferranti, "The Nazi-Loving Drug Lord Who Revolutionized the Cocaine Smuggling Industry;" Ron Chepesiuk, *Crazy Charlie: Carlos Lehder, Revolutionary or Neo Nazi* (Rock Hill, SC: Strategic Media Books, 2016).
16. Mark Bowden, *Killing Pablo: The Hunt for the World's Greatest Outlaw* (New York, NY: Penguin Books, 2002); Ernesto Dal Bó, Pedro Dal Bó, and Rafael Di Tella, "'Plata o Plomo?': bribe and punishment in a theory of political influence," *American Political Science Review* 100, no. 1 (2006): pp. 41–53.
17. For more, see: "Sebastian Marroquín's Reflections on Pablo Escobar—60 Minutes," *60 Minutes*, Jun 1, 2017, https://www.youtube.com/watch?v=pNuKlunRt_k&t=125s, accessed June 29, 2020; "Interview with Sebastian Marroquin (the son of Pablo Escobar)," *SVT/NRK/Skavlan*, March 10, 2017, https://www.youtube.com/watch?v=068VCJNEsOw, accessed June 29, 2020; Juan Pablo Escobar, translated by Andrea Rosenberg, *Pablo Escobar: My Father* (New York, NY: Thomas Dunne Books, 2016).
18. Adam Isacson, "Making Sense of Colombia's 'Post-Conflcit' Conflict," in *The Criminalization of States: The Relationship between States and Organized Crime*, eds. Jonathan D. Rosen, Bruce Bagley, and Jorge Chabat (Lanham, MD: Lexington Books, 2019), p. 210.
19. Adam Isacson, "Making Sense of Colombia's 'Post-Conflcit' Conflict."
20. Associated Press, "Justice Minister Slain in Bogota," *The New York Times*, May 1, 1984.
21. Benjamin Lessing, *Making Peace in Drug Wars: Crackdowns and Cartels in Latin America*; David P. Thompson, "Pablo Escobar, drug baron: his surrender, imprisonment, and escape," *Studies in Conflict & Terrorism* 19, no. 1 (1996): pp. 55–91; Mark Andrew Sherman, "United States International Drug Control Policy, Extradition, and the Rule of Law in Colombia," *Nova Law Review* 15 (1991): p. 661; Rensselaer W. Lee, "Cocaine mafia," *Society* 27, no. 2 (1990): pp. 53–62.

22. For more, see: Jeremy W. Coid, "The Federal Administrative Maximum Penitentiary, Florence, Colorado," *Medicine, Science and the Law* 41, no. 4 (2001): pp. 287–297; Robert Perkinson, "Shackled justice: Florence Federal Penitentiary and the new politics of punishment," *Social Justice* 21, no. 3 (57 (1994): pp. 117–132.
23. John Lee Anderson, "The Afterlife of Pablo Escobar: In Colombia, a drug lord's posthumous celebrity brings profits and controversy," *The New Yorker*, February 26, 2018; Joseph B. Treaster, "Drug Baron Gives Up in Colombia As End to Extradition Is Approved," *The New York Times*, June 20, 1991; Bruce Bagley, "Carteles de la droga: de Medellín a Sinaloa," *Criterios* 4, no. 1 (2011): pp. 233–247.
24. Kyra Gurney, "Latin America's Top 5 Prison Parties," InSight Crime, October 27, 2014, https://www.insightcrime.org/news/analysis/latin-america-top-five-prison-parties/, accessed May 14, 2020; Patrick Naef, "'Narco-heritage' and the Touristification of the Drug Lord Pablo Escobar in Medellin, Colombia," *Journal of Anthropological Research* 74, no. 4 (2018): pp. 485–502; John D. Martz, "Colombia: Democracy, development, and drugs," *Current History* 93, no. 581 (1994): p. 134.
25. James Bargent, *Colombia's Mirror: War and Drug Trafficking in the Prison System* (Washington, DC: InSight Crime, 2017); David P. Thompson, "Pablo Escobar, drug baron: his surrender, imprisonment, and escape; Patrick. Naef, "'Narco-heritage' and the Touristification of the Drug Lord Pablo Escobar in Medellin, Colombia," *Journal of Anthropological Research* 74, no. 4 (2018): pp. 485–502.
26. Steve Murphy and Javier F. Peña, *Manhunters: How We Took Down Pablo Escobar* (New York, NY: St Martin's Press, 2019).
27. For more, see: Juan Pablo Escobar, translated by Andrea Rosenberg, *Pablo Escobar: My Father* (New York, NY: St. Martin's Press, 2016); Steve Murphy and Javier F. Peña, *Manhunters: How We Took Down Pablo Escobar*.
28. U.S. Department of Justice (DOJ), *The Cali Cartel: The New Kings of Cocaine*.
29. Bruce Bagley, *Drug Trafficking and Organized Crime in the Americas: Major Trends in the Twenty-First Century* (Washington, DC: Woodrow Wilson Center International Center for Scholars, 2012); Benjamin. Lessing, "The logic of violence in criminal war: Cartel-state conflict in Mexico, Colombia, and Brazil," PhD dissertation, UC Berkeley, 2012; R. Nieves, "Colombian cocaine cartels: Lessons from the front," *Trends in Organized Crime* 3, no. 3 (1998): pp. 13–29.
30. Nicolás Espinosa and Daniel Ruiz, "Caminando el despeje," *Análisis Político* 44 (2001): pp. 91–103; Russell Crandall, "Clinton, Bush and Plan Colombia," *Survival* 44, no. 1 (2002): pp. 159–172; Daniel García-Pena, "The National Liberation Army (ELN) creates a different peace process,"

NACLA Report on the Americas 34, no. 2 (2000): p. 34; Adam Isacson, "Colombia peace in tatters," *NACLA Report on the Americas* 35, no. 5 (2002): pp. 10–13; Andrei Gomez-Suarez and Jonathan Newman, "Safeguarding Political Guarantees in the Colombian Peace Process: have Santos and FARC learnt the lessons from the past?" *Third World Quarterly* 34, no. 5 (2013): pp. 819–837; Andres Cala, "The enigmatic guerrilla: FARC's Manuel Marulanda," *Current History* 99, no. 634 (2000): p. 56; Nazih Richani, "The politics of negotiating peace in Colombia," *NACLA Report on the Americas* 38, no. 6 (2005): pp. 17–22; Alfredo Molano, "The Evolution of the FARC: A guerrilla group's long history," *NACLA Report on the Americas* 34, no. 2 (2000): pp. 23–31.

31. For more, see: Chester G. Oehme, "Plan Colombia: reassessing the strategic framework," *Democracy and Security* 6, no. 3 (2010): pp. 221–236; William M. LeoGrande and Kenneth E. Sharpe, "Two Wars or One? Drugs, Guerrillas, and Colombia's New 'Violencia,'" *World Policy Journal* 17, no. 3 (2000): pp. 1–11.

32. For more, see: Jonathan D. Rosen, *The Losing War: Plan Colombia and Beyond* (Albany, NY: State University of New York Press, 2014); Jonathan D. Rosen, "The war on drugs in Colombia: A current account of U.S. policy," *Perspectivas Internacionales*, Vol. 9, No. 2 (2013): pp. 58–83; James Petras, "Geopolitics of plan Colombia," *Economic and Political Weekly* (2000): pp. 4617–4623; Michael Shifter, "Plan Colombia: A Retrospective," *Americas Quarterly* 6, no. 3 (2012): p. 36; Doug Stokes, "Better lead than bread? A critical analysis of the US's plan Colombia," *Civil Wars* 4, no. 2 (2001): pp. 59–78.

33. Office of the Press Secretary, "President Bush and President Uribe of Colombia Participate in a Joint Press Availability," *The White House*, March 11, 2007, p. 4.

34. Adam Isacson, "Making Sense of Colombia's 'Post-Conflict' Conflict," in *The Criminalization of State: The Relationship between States and Organized Crime*, eds. Jonathan D. Rosen, Bruce Bagley, and Jorge Chabat (Lanham, MD: Lexington Books, 2019), pp. 209–227.

35. For more, see: Michelle L. Dion and Catherine Russler, "Eradication efforts, the state, displacement and poverty: Explaining coca cultivation in Colombia during Plan Colombia," *Journal of Latin American Studies* 40, no. 3 (2008): pp. 399–421.

36. Adriana Camacho, and Daniel Mejia, "The health consequences of aerial spraying illicit crops: The case of Colombia," *Journal of Health Economics* 54 (2017): pp. 147–160; Ricardo Vargas, "The anti-drug policy, aerial spraying of illicit crops and their social, environmental and political impacts in Colombia," *Journal of Drug Issues* 32, no. 1 (2002): pp. 11–60.

37. Adam Isacson, "Restarting Aerial Fumigation of Drug Crops in Colombia is a Mistake," *Washington Office on Latin America*, March 7, 2019, https://www.wola.org/analysis/restarting-aerial-fumigation-of-drug-crops-in-colombia-is-a-mistake/, accessed April 4, 2019, p. 3.
38. For more, see: Jonathan D. Rosen, *The Losing War: Plan Colombia and Beyond* (Albany, NY: State University of New York Press, 2014); Marten W. Brienen, "Bolivian Drug Policy under the Morales Administration," in *Drug trafficking, Organized Crime, and Violence in the Americas Today*, eds. Bruce M. Bagley and Jonathan D. Rosen (Gainesville, FL, University Press of Florida, 2015), pp. 203–222.
39. United Nations Offices on Drugs and Crime (UNODC), Colombia: Coca cultivation survey 2009 (Bogotá, CO: UNODC, 2010).
40. Winifred Tate, "US human rights activism and plan Colombia," *Colombia Internacional* 69 (2009): pp. 50–69.
41. Quoted in Michael Evans, ed. "Former Colombian President's Ranch Was Paramilitary Base, According to New Testimony," *National Security Archive at George Washington University*, Jul 9, 2018, https://nsarchive.gwu.edu/news/colombia/2018-07-09/former-colombian-presidents-ranch-paramilitary-base-according-new-testimony, accessed May 14, 2020.
42. United States Attorney's Office Southern District of Florida, "High-level Colombian Bacrim Narco-trafficker indicted on cocaine conspiracy charges," *United States Attorney's Office Southern District of Florida*, February 9, 2011.
43. InSight Crime, "Rastrojos," *InSight Crime*, February 16, 2017, https://www.insightcrime.org/colombia-organized-crime-news/rastrojos-profile/, May 14, 2020; Carlos Andrés. Prieto, "Bandas criminales en Colombia:¿ amenaza a la seguridad regional?" *Revista opera* 12 (2012): pp. 181–204.
44. The United States Attorney's Office Eastern District of New York, "Ten Alleged Members of a Colombian Drug Trafficking Organization Charged with Distributing over 25,000 Kilograms of Cocaine," *The United States Attorney's Office Eastern District of New York*, June 07, 2011.
45. Quoted in The United States Attorney's Office Eastern District of New York, "Ten Alleged Members of a Colombian Drug Trafficking Organization Charged with Distributing over 25,000 Kilograms of Cocaine."
46. Marc Chernick interview in Jonathan D. Rosen, *The Losing War: Plan Colombia and Beyond*; for more of Chernick's work, see: Marc Chernick, "The paramilitarization of the war in Colombia," *NACLA Report on the Americas* 31, no. 5 (1998): pp. 28–33; Marc W. Chernick, "Negotiated settlement to armed conflict: Lessons from the Colombian peace process,"

Journal of Interamerican Studies and World Affairs 30, no. 4 (1988): pp. 53–88.
47. James Bargent and Mat Charles, "InSide Colombia's BACRIM: Power," *InSight Crime*, July 13, 2017, https://www.insightcrime.org/investigations/inside-colombia-s-bacrim-power/, accessed May 14, 2020.
48. U.S. Department of State, "Narcotics Rewards Program: Dario Antonio Usuga David," *U.S. Department of State*, https://2009-2017.state.gov/j/inl/narc/rewards/188937.htm, accessed May 14, 2020.
49. Nicholas Casey, "Colombia's President, Juan Manuel Santos, Is Awarded Nobel Peace Prize," *The New York Times*, October 7, 2016.
50. For more on the FARC demobilization, see: Enzo Nussio and Kimberly Howe, "What if the FARC Demobilizes?" *Stability: International Journal of Security & Development* 1, no. 1 (2012): pp. 58–67.
51. Melissa Velásquez Loaiza, "'FARCrim', las nuevas bandas criminales que controlan el negocio de las drogas en el sur de Colombia, según informe," *CNN*, March 15, 2018.
52. Drug Enforcement Administration (DEA) *Colombian Cocaine Production Expansion Contributes to Rise in Supply in the United States* (Springfield, VA: DEA, 2017).
53. Quoted in Jeremy McDermott, "Op-Ed: Duque 'Has Done Nothing for Us,' Says Trump," *InSight Crime*, April 6, 2019, https://www.insightcrime.org/news/analysis/duque-done-nothing-trump-us-colombia/, accessed May 21, 2020.
54. Jeremy McDermott, "Op-Ed: Duque 'Has Done Nothing for Us,' Says Trump," p. 3.
55. Quoted in Reuters, "Colombia will have to restart aerial spraying to destroy coca: Trump," *Reuters*, March 2, 2020.
56. Washington Office on Latin America (WOLA), "U.S.-Colombia Anti-Drug Plan Pushes Failed Policy of Aerial Fumigation," *WOLA*, March 6, 2020, https://www.wola.org/2020/03/usa-colombia-anti-drug-plan-failed-aerial-fumigation/, accessed May 15, 2020, p. 1.
57. Washington Office on Latin America (WOLA), "Colombia Pushes Coca Eradication During COVID-19 Pandemic," *WOLA*, April 23, 2020, https://www.wola.org/2020/04/colombia-covid19-coca-eradication/, accessed May 15, 2020.
58. Washington Office on Latin America (WOLA), "Colombia Pushes Coca Eradication During COVID-19 Pandemic."
59. Jeremy McDermott, "The 'Invisibles': Colombia's New Generation of Drug Traffickers," *InSight Crime*, March 15, 2018, https://www.insightcrime.org/investigations/invisibles-colombias-new-generation-drug-traffickers/, accessed May 14, 2020.

60. For more, see: Jonathan Daniel Rosen and Roberto Zepeda Martínez, "La guerra contra las drogas en Colombia y México: estrategias fracasadas," *Ánfora*, Vol. 21, No. 38 (2014): pp. 179–200; Jonathan D. Rosen, Bruce Bagley, and Jorge Chabat, eds., *The Criminalization of States: The Relationship Between States and Organized Crime* (Lanham, MD: Lexington Books, 2019); Ambos Kai, "Impunity and International Criminal Law: A Case Study on Colombia, Peru, Bolivia, Chile and Argentina," *Human Rights Law Journal* 18 (1997): pp. 1–15; Javier Giraldo, "Corrupted justice and the schizophrenic state in Colombia," *Social Justice* 26, no. 4 vol. 78 (1999): pp. 31–54; Elvira Maria Restrepo, Fabio Sánchez, and Mariana Martínez Cuéllar, "Impunity or punishment? An analysis of criminal investigation into kidnapping, terrorism and embezzlement in Colombia," *Global Crime* 7, no. 2 (2006): pp. 176–199; Javaria Ahmad, "The Colombian Law of Justice and Peace: One Step Further from Peace and One Step Closer to Impunity," *Transnat'l L. & Contemp. Probs.* 16 (2006): p. 333.

CHAPTER 3

Drug Trafficking and Organized Crime in Mexico

Abstract This chapter examines drug trafficking and organized crime in Mexico. It begins with a history of drug trafficking and how it has evolved over time. It focuses on the 71-year rule by a single political party and the transition to democracy in 2000, which had an impact on the relationship between the state and organized crime. This chapter then examines Felipe Calderón's war on drugs and the Mérida Initiative, a U.S.-funded plan, to help the Mexican government combat drug trafficking and organized crime. It then examines recent trends in drug trafficking, organized crime, and counternarcotic policies, focusing on the Peña Nieto and López Obrador governments. It examines opium production and the evolution of organized crime in the State of Guerrero. Finally, this chapter analyzes the impact of the Coronavirus on organized crime and the challenges combating corruption and impunity.

Keywords Mérida Initiative • Felipe Calderón • Enrique Peña Nieto • Corruption • Impunity • Violence

In 2018, the Texas-born Edgar Valdez Villarreal, known as "La Barbie," received more than 49 years in federal prison for his role in drug trafficking. According to Byung J. Pak, a U.S. Attorney, "Valdez-Villareal imported tons of cocaine into the US while ruthlessly working his way up the ranks of one of Mexico's most powerful cartels, leaving in his wake countless lives destroyed by drugs and violence."[1] In the late 1990s, the former high school football player moved to Mexico after facing drug charges in the United States. He moved up the ranks of the Beltran Leyva Organization until his capture in 2010.[2] This chapter examines some of the recent trends in drug trafficking, violence, and the government's efforts to combat drug kingpins, such as "La Barbie." It begins with a historical overview of the relationship between the state and organized crime during the more than seven decades of single-party rule. It then explains the impact that the transition to democracy has had on the country's institutions. This chapter then turns to Felipe Calderón's war on drugs and the consequences of the militarization strategy. Calderón left office with more than 100,000 drug-related deaths. It also examines President Enrique Peña Nieto and his administration's security policies and the impact on drug-related violence. It concludes by addressing the challenges that the current president faces as he inherited a country tired of violence, human rights abuses, and corruption. Today, Mexico is experiencing historic levels of violence, and there is a need for major institutional and policy reforms.

The History of Drug Trafficking and Organized Crime

Mexican criminal organizations have evolved over time. These criminal organizations are more sophisticated today and have diversified their illicit activities, such as human trafficking, money laundering, extortion, and stealing oil. This is a drastic change as 90 years ago criminal groups consisted of family clans that trafficked liquor and marijuana to the United States.[3] Opium traffickers were Chinese immigrants that lived in the north of Mexico.[4] Interestingly, the Chinese were less involved in marijuana trafficking. These smugglers were family units operating small-scale operations as opposed to large criminal groups.[5]

Marijuana and opiates have been trafficked from Mexico to the United States since the late 1940s, when individuals, like Enrique Diarte, trafficked illicit drugs through Tijuana and Mexicali to the United States. Enrique Fernández Puerta, often referred to as the Al Capone of Ciudad Juárez, also participated in an assortment of illicit activities during this same time period, utilizing the proximity of Ciudad Juárez to the United States to move a variety of products from bootlegged alcohol to drugs.[6]

Jorge Chabat, a Mexican security expert, notes that drug trafficking did not represent a "major consideration" for U.S.-Mexican bilateral relations until the 1970s.[7] Tensions increased between the United States and Mexico when drug traffickers captured, tortured, and killed Enrique "Kiki" Camarena, a 37-year-old Drug Enforcement Administration (DEA) agent, in 1985.[8] The United States accused a medical doctor, Humberto Álvarez Macháin, of helping keep Camarena alive while the assailants tortured him.[9] A witness testified in court that he witnessed Mexican government officials enter and leave meetings where people planned the operation to capture Camarena.[10] The traffickers' involvement in this crime increased the pressure of the U.S. government on Mexico. The leading political party for seven decades let traffickers operate with impunity during this period if they remained "low profile." As Peter Watt and Roberto Zepeda contend, "So long as the DEA did not overly pressurise the Mexicans, and traffickers were shrewd enough to stay out of the public eye, impunity for murder and smuggling was frequently assured."[11] The death of Camarena crossed the line, and the U.S. government responded to the disappearance of this young DEA agent by launching a second phase of a plan known as "Operation Intercept," with the goal of increasing border security and decreasing the trafficking of illicit drugs as well as contraband across the U.S.-Mexico border.[12]

Agent Camarena's murder led to the arrest of drug trafficking kingpins, including Rueben Zuno Arce, Rafael Caro Quintero, and Miguel Felix Gallardo, among others.[13] Zuno Arce's involvement in the torture and death of Camarena further strained bilateral relations between the U.S. and the Mexican government as he had political connections at the highest level of government; he was the brother-in-law of Luis Echeverría Álvarez, the president between 1970 and 1976. Ultimately, Zuno received two life sentences and died while in federal prison at the age of 82.[14]

The capture of the Guadalajara cartel leaders had significant consequences for the drug trafficking and organized crime landscape. The arrest of Miguel Ángel Félix Gallardo caused the drug traffickers to divide the territory controlled by the Guadalajara cartel to other cartel members. This led to a fragmentation of the organized crime landscape as the Guadalajara cartel previously dominated the criminal underworld. Benjamin Lessing, a drug trafficking expert at the University of Chicago, notes: "While Gallardo originally intended this to prevent succession battles, the end result was the fragmentation of Guadalajara's near monopoly into an oligopolistic market of powerful cartel-clans."[15] Thus, the splintering of the cartel changed the evolution and landscape of organized crime in Mexico.

While drug traffickers battled for control of territory, economic integration and globalization helped drug trafficking and organized crime groups during the 1990s. The United States, Mexico, and Canada signed the North American Free Trade Agreement (NAFTA), which went into effect in 1994. Free trade and interconnectedness increased linkages between the North American countries. Illicit traffickers took advantage of the improvements in infrastructure, ease of shipping, and commerce to move drugs from Mexico to the United States.[16] Drug traffickers, for instance, could transport drugs in trucks and vehicles from Mexico to the United States, and it is impossible for U.S. authorities to inspect every car or truck passing the border due to the sheer number of drugs crossing the border every day. Traffickers, therefore, have taken advantage of the improved infrastructure and interconnectedness between the North American countries.

The PRI, Organized Crime, and the Transition

Drug trafficking and organized crime in Mexico cannot be understood without analyzing the evolution of the political system. The Institutional Revolutionary Party (Partido Revolucionario Institucional—PRI) dominated Mexico's political landscape for more than seven decades. The PRI negotiated with drug trafficking organizations, which helped enrich corrupt officials.[17] While the relationship between the PRI and organized crime fueled corruption, lack of transparency, and high levels of impunity, it also impacted the levels of violence. The PRI maintained tight control on organized crime, which helped keep violence in-check.[18]

The relationship between the state and organized crime evolved as a result of several important factors. First, the PRI's domination of Mexico's federal government (i.e., municipal, state, and federal level) began to breakdown in the 1980s when the PRI lost control of Baja California when the National Action Party (Partido Acción Nacional—PAN) won the gubernatorial election. Second, Colombian traffickers became more involved in Mexico, increasing the number of criminal actors operating in the country. The PRI could easily negotiate with several major criminal organizations, but it became much more difficult as the number of criminal groups increased. Organized crime associations do not want to receive fewer advantages from corrupt PRI officials. The increasing number of actors changed the rules of the game and the ability of the government to use its leverage to cut deals. In other words, the negotiating process becomes much more complex as the number of groups involved in the criminal underworld spikes. Finally, a restructuring of the jurisdictions as well as territorial control of the Attorney General's office Procuraduría General de la República—PGR) occurred in 1996. The country also experienced various reforms and prosecutorial initiatives, which led to changes in the ability of the PGR to fight drug trafficking and organized crime.[19]

In 2000, Vicente Fox of the PAN won the presidential election. This election represented a watershed moment, as there must be alterations in political parties for a country to be defined as a democracy. The Fox administration represented an opportunity for Mexico to strengthen institutions through serious structural reforms designed to address the high levels of corruption and impunity plaguing the political landscape.[20] Yet the administration had a difficult time changing decades of inertia, and Mexico was plagued the same institutions prior to the transition.

Felipe Calderón assumed the presidency in 2006. He won in a highly contested election against Andrés Manuel López Obrador, known as AMLO. Protesters took the streets to voice their disapproval of the election results as many Mexicans believed that the PAN manipulated the votes.[21] Calderón assumed office with high levels of illegitimacy. He sought to consolidate power and demonstrate his leadership capacity. The newly minted president launched a war on drugs to combat insecurity, drug trafficking, and organized crime. Calderón deployed the military to his home state of Michoacán. Critics, however, contend that the military should not be utilized in internal security operations. In the United States, for instance, the Posse Comitatus Act prevents the military from patrolling the streets. President Calderón utilized the military because he had high levels of distrust in the police forces. Survey data show that the Mexican police are highly distrusted by the public. The most distrusted police force is the local police as they are the most corrupt given that there is less oversight, transparency, and accountability at the municipal level. On the other hand, the armed forces are perceived as more professional and better trained. They are one of the most trusted institutions in Mexico,[22] and Calderón utilized the better-trained security forces to combat organized crime.

The Mexican government received support from the U.S. government through the Mérida Initiative.[23] The plan, originally known as Plan Mexico, changes its name, in part to disassociate it from Plan Colombia.

The Mérida Initiative focused on four pillars, but the first pillar constituted the most important element of the plan. While there are differences between Plan Colombia and the Mérida Initiative, this initiative has focused on capturing the leaders of organized crime groups. In addition, most of the resources supported the military and police. Skeptics, however, contend that this plan constitutes a militarized approach to combating drug trafficking and organized crime. They maintain that it does not address many of the underlying issues, such as corruption and impunity.[24]

PILLAR ONE – Disrupt Capacity of Organized Crime to Operate

Diminish the power of Mexican organized criminal groups by systematically capturing and incarcerating their leaders and by reducing drug trade revenues by interdicting drugs, stopping money laundering, and diminishing production. Through equipment, technology, and training, the Merida Initiative will support better investigations, more captures and arrests, successful prosecutions, and shipment interdiction.

PILLAR TWO – Institutionalize Capacity to Sustain Rule of Law

Enhance the capacity of Mexican public security, border and judicial institutions to sustain the rule of law. Merida Initiative programs will strengthen the capabilities of key institutions to improve internal controls, further professionalize the military and police, reform corrections institutions, and assist in the transition to the New Criminal Justice System.

PILLAR THREE – Create a 21st Century Border Structure

Facilitate legitimate commerce and movement of people while curtailing the illicit flow of drugs, people, arms, and cash. The Merida Initiative will provide the foundation for better infrastructure and technology to strengthen and modernize border security at northern and southern land crossings, ports, and airports. Professionalization programs will transfer new skills to the agencies managing the border and additional non-intrusive technologies will assist in the detection of criminal activities.

PILLAR FOUR – Build Strong and Resilient Communities

Strengthen communities by creating a culture of lawfulness and undercutting the lure and power of drug trafficking organizations. By implementing job creation programs, engaging youth in their communities, expanding social safety nets, and building community confidence in public institutions, Merida Initiative assistance will test new initiatives to strengthen Mexican communities against organized crime.[25]

The Calderón administration focused on capturing the leaders of criminal organizations and increased the number of extraditions as the United States pursued many of the key drug trafficking leaders for federal crimes. In 2006, for instance, Mexico extradited 63 people to the United States. In 2008, the number of Mexicans extradited increased to 95. In 2009, the number of extraditions spiked to 107. While nationalism could have prevented extraditions, the Calderón administration cooperated with the requests of the U.S. government.[26]

The Mérida Initiative also supported the Mexican military and police and provided equipment and training. The funding of the initiative came from International Narcotics Control and Law Enforcement (INCLE), Foreign Military Financing (FMF), and Economic Support Fund (ESF). The funding increased from $48.1 million in FY 2007 to $639.2 million by FY 2010. The Obama administration continued to support the Mérida Initiative. However, it relaunched the endeavor and sought to help combat crime in Central America through the Central America Regional Security Initiative (CARSI), as will be discussed in more detail below.[27]

One of the major consequences of the Calderón administration's war on drugs has been the fragmentation of organized crime. The country had four dominant cartels in 2006 when Calderón assumed office: the Juárez/Vicente Carillo Fuentes Organization (CFO), the Sinaloa cartel, and the Tijuana/Arellano Felix organization (AFO). By 2007, Mexico had eight major cartels. By 2010, the number of cartels increased to 12 organizations.[28] Experts disagree about the number of drug trafficking organizations as some people contend that there are nine major drug trafficking groups, while other analysts indicate that there are 20.[29] In 2012, the Attorney General of Mexico contended that the country had 80 drug trafficking organizations.[30]

Eduardo Guerrero-Gutiérrez, a Mexican security expert, indicates that cartels can be placed into four categories: national cartels, "toll collector" cartels, regional cartels, and local mafias.[31] Today, the national category could be replaced with transnational as it consists of organizations that control different drug trafficking *plazas* and are diversifying their revenue streams across international borders. The "toll collector" cartel, as the name implies, consists of criminal groups like the Tijuana cartel that obtain income from charging "tolls" on drugs and commodities that move through their territory. These organizations operate in various border areas that are essential crossing points for trafficking illicit commodities. The regional cartels consist of groups like the Knights Templar. These organizations can best be described as playing a "secondary role" in the drug trade in certain zones.[32] They are less powerful than the national cartels. Finally, there are "local mafias," such as the Cartel of Acapulco, that are the result of fragmentations from larger criminal organizations like the Beltrán Leyva Organization (BLO).

The transnational category includes criminal organizations like the Sinaloa cartel. The Sinaloa cartel is one of the most powerful transnational organized crime groups in the Western Hemisphere. The Sinaloa cartel, which was led by Joaquín "El Chapo" Guzmán, until his extradition to the United States, is present in more than 15 Mexican states and as many as 50 countries, which has enabled the organization to generate billions of dollars in revenue.[33] The cartel is less hierarchical than perceived and operates like a franchise system. In fact, some experts have maintained that the cartel functions more like Walmart or McDonalds and utilizes this franchise system to dominate the criminal underworld in many countries throughout the region. Tom Wainwright contends, "The theory is that the cartels in the area have what economists call a 'monopsony,' [which is] like a monopoly on buying in the area." According to Wainwright, "This rang a bell with me because it's something that people very often say about Wal-Mart."[34] The cartel works with local partners in other countries, enabling it to increase its power and control over the supply chain.

The Sinaloa cartel has learned the lessons—both successes and failures—from other drug trafficking organizations, such as Colombia's Cali cartel, which operated with less violence than its rival Medellín cartel and utilized its ability to influence political actors through bribes and obtain outcomes that benefited the operations of the Cali criminal enterprise. Learning from the Cali cartel, the Sinaloa cartel has focused on developing intricate connections with government leaders through bribes and other corrupt practices. The cartel has managed to cultivate close connections with high-level government and security officials. Many analysts note that the Sinaloa cartel has had better relationships with the PAN than other political parties.[35] In December 2019, for instance, U.S. authorities indicted Genaro Garcia Luna, the former Secretary of Public Security in Mexico during the six years of the Calderón administration, on various criminal counts, including conspiracy to traffic cocaine. The U.S. Attorney for the Eastern District of New York, Richard P. Donoghue, stated: "Garcia Luna stands accused of taking millions of dollars in bribes from 'El Chapo' Guzman's Sinaloa Cartel while he controlled Mexico's Federal Police Force and was responsible for ensuring public safety in Mexico."[36]

The sentence carries the possibility of a maximum of life in prison for Garcia Luna, who was living in Florida at the time of his arrest.[37] This arrest demonstrates the capacity of the Sinaloa cartel to use its power and resources to penetrate the state apparatus in order to bribe high level security officials.

While the Sinaloa cartel infiltrated the Mexican state through its corrupt acts, fighting between cartels and government strategies led to spikes in violence. President Calderón claimed that 90 percent of the deaths during his administration resulted from people involved in drug trafficking and organized crime. He contended, "the vast majority, more than 90 percent, (of the violent deaths have occurred) in actions by criminals against other criminals; the vast majority (of attacks) are not even against the authorities, much less so against civilians and much, much less so against tourists."[38] Critics disputed these assertions and highlighted the number of journalists, politicians, and targeted killings of women. The number of mayors and former mayors, for instance, increased from one in 2006 to nine in 2009. By 2010, Mexico had 17 current and former mayors killed. In 2008, for example, seven journalists or media-support workers were killed. This number increased to 14 in 2010 and 19 in 2011, revealing that it is very dangerous to be a journalist in Mexico as organized crime groups do not want publicity about their operations and can silence opposition through torture and death.[39]

President Calderón left office with the country hampered by drug trafficking, organized crime, and violence.[40] The focus on capturing the major cartel leaders and marketing the victories to the public did not decrease the number of criminal organizations operating in the country. In fact, it is the opposite: the deployment of the military and the capturing of drug kingpins caused cartels to fragment and increased the number of groups operating in Mexico. The militarization of the drug war led to spikes in homicides as criminal groups battled with the military and among each other for control of the lucrative criminal underworld.

The end of the Calderón administration and the failed war on drugs strategies paved the way for a new president to address many of the underlying structural problems that have enabled drug traffickers to flourish—principally state weakness, corruption, and impunity. The new president had the opportunity to focus not only on de-militarizing the drug war but also on implementing deep-seated structural reforms to the police, the penitentiary system, as well as the legislative and judicial branches of government.

ENRIQUE PEÑA NIETO: CRIME, VIOLENCE, AND CORRUPTION

President Enrique Peña Nieto, the young star of the PRI, assumed office in 2018 and pledged to change the drug war strategy. President Peña Nieto stressed the need to make reforms to various government sectors. While he changed the discourse of the war on drugs, many critics argue that his policies remained very similar to his predecessor.[41] Peña Nieto continued to utilize the armed forces because of the high levels of distrust in the police.

Like the Calderón administration, the Peña Nieto government focused on capturing the kingpins. Upon assuming office, Peña Nieto created a list of 122 criminals that his government would focus its energy and resources on capturing. By the end of the administration, the government had "neutralized" 110 of the individuals on this list. Of the list, 96 people had been arrested, with 28 from the Zetas and 21 from the Sinaloa cartel. The arrests also included members from the Jalisco New Generation Cartel, Beltrán Levya Organization, Gulf cartel, and Juárez cartel. Fourteen of the 122 people on this list died during operations that led to confrontations with security units. This list also included nine people sentenced by the court system. Finally, 3 of the 122 were extradited to the United States.[42]

The capturing of the drug kingpins was touted by the Peña Nieto government as a victory for Mexico, but there have been collateral consequences. The kingpin strategy can result in increases in violence as the toppling of one leader can create tensions within an organization for control. In addition, rival organizations can compete for control of routes and territory. This could lead to increased levels of violence, which is something that the Peña Nieto administration witnessed.

While the Peña Nieto administration sought to recast the Mérida Initiative,[43] critics argue that the Mérida Initiative has not been effective in addressing organized crime and violence. Anna Grace maintains, "Fighting fire with fire has led to an escalation in the number of deaths in Mexico since the initiative began. Kingpins have fallen, yet major transnational criminal organizations remain at large."[44] The capturing of leaders has also led to infighting within cartels and between different organizations. Thus, while some kingpins have been captured or killed, the drug market remains the same and violence began to increase.

Violence initially dropped during the Peña Nieto administration, but it later increased over time. In 2013, for example, the country recorded more than 23,000 deaths. The number declined to 20,010 in 2014, but the number of murders increased to 24,559 in 2016. By 2017, Mexico recorded more than 32,000 deaths, representing a dramatic increase in the number of deaths. President Peña Nieto finished his presidency with more than 150,000 deaths during his six years in office (Fig. 3.1).[45]

Violence during the Peña Nieto government impacted many parts of the country, as opposed to only certain border towns, not only because of fighting among organized crime groups for control of routes and territory, but also because of the deployment of the military to different zones in the country. By the end of the Peña Nieto government, the southern state of Guerrero, for example, recorded more than 13,900 executions, while the State of Mexico had more than 17,200 deaths. Jalisco, Michoacán, and Guanajuato recorded 8749, 7332 and 8797 deaths, respectively.

Moreover, the Peña Nieto government had intricate relationships between the state and criminal groups, exemplified by the events that transpired in 2014 in the southern state of Guerrero. Students from a rural teachers college named Escuela Normal Rural Raúl Isidro Burgos would commandeer buses and travel to Mexico City to protest. In

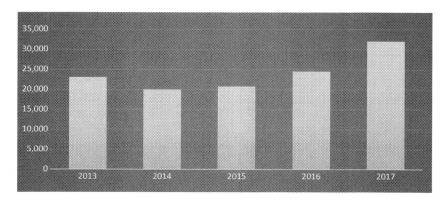

Fig. 3.1 Number of deaths in Mexico (2013–2017). (Source: Created by author with data from *Proceso*)

September 2014, the police in the town of Iguala surrounded a bus of students from Ayotzinapa. The officers stated, "We're going to kill all of you."[46] The Mexican government's account is that the police shot and turned over students to a local gang known as Guerreros Unidos. This criminal organization is a result of the splintering of the Beltrán Leyva Organization that is involved in kidnapping, extortion, and drug trafficking.[47] The official version of the Mexican government is that the federal police did not have any involvement in this case. Yet according to Anabel Hernández, a leading Mexican journalist, the government has continually lied about the events that transpired. She contends, "Well, the students arrive near Iguala. The army, the Federal Police, the state police were waiting for them." Hernández asserts that the students, unknowingly, had commandeered buses used for transporting heroin: "According with my investigation, the first responsible (sic) of this crime was the 27th Battalion in Iguala, in particular, the colonel that received the phone call from the drug lord ordering him. You have to rescue my drugs. I pay you for this. You have – I don't know what you have to do. I want my drugs back."[48] This is the real motivation, according to some experts, behind the killing of the 43 students as they stole the wrong bus at the wrong time.

The Mexican public has demanded justice for the 43 missing students from Ayotzinapa, but critics maintain that the Peña Nieto administration mismanaged the crisis. Authorities arrested the mayor of Iguala and his wife,[49] but the Mexican government's account of what happened did not align with the versions of the outside investigators. Five experts named by the Inter-American Commission on Human Rights (IACHR) to study this case consulted with fire analysts and indicated that it was unlikely that the bodies of the students were burned at a trash dumping site.[50] The United Nations conducted a report to examine what happened to the 43 students and the Mexican government's handling of this situation. Zeid Ra'ad al-Hussein, the United Nations High Commissioner for Human Rights, stated: "The findings of the report point to a pattern of committing, tolerating and covering up torture in the investigation of the Ayotzinapa case."[51] The Peña Nieto government attempted to obstruct justice and tamper with evidence, which only increased levels of support for the need to reform judicial institutions[52] and combat the high levels of corruption present across institutions at the three levels of government.

The events in Guerrero have caused pain for countless families who are demanding justice for the missing students. Cristina Bautista Salvador, the mother of Benjamin, maintains hope. Cristina, whose native language is

Náhuatl, learned Spanish after the disappearance of her son so she could speak about the case to lawyers and shed light to this tragic event. She contended, "Whether there be many or few, nationally or internationally, we'll keep pushing until we find out what happened." She remains determined to find the truth, stating: "Until we find them."[53] Like Bautista Salvador Emiliano Navarrete Victoriano, the father of José Ángel Navarrete González, who was 18 at the time of his disappearance, has continued to search in spite of all the pain and trauma: "At this point I don't care what I lose as long as I find him."[54] As of June 2020, progress has remained slow and the Mexican government is no closer to getting to the bottom of the events that transpired in 2014.

The events that occurred in Guerrero have only increased levels of distrust in the government and its ability to ensure human rights. According to the 2016/2017 LAPOP data, 70.58 percent of Mexicans responded "very little" when asked the level of protection of human rights today in Mexico, while only 6.99 percent stated "too much." Moreover, 22.75 percent answered "not at all" when asked if basic rights are protected in Mexico, while only 4.63 percent answered "a lot."

President Peña Nieto's popularity continued to decline after several other scandals, including the escape of "El Chapo" Guzmán. In February 2014, Mexican soldiers moved through Mazatlán, Sinaloa, responding to a tip about Guzmán, who had been on the run since he escaped from prison in 2001 through a laundry basket. Indeed, the initial capture of Guzmán represented a major victory for the Mexican government. During the arrest of the billionaire drug kingpin, authorities seized a plethora of weapons, including 2 grenade launchers, 36 handguns, 97 large guns, a rocket launcher, and dozens of cars.[55] For years, the U.S. government had been requesting the extradition of Guzmán for a litany of federal crimes. The Mexican government, however, refused to extradite him and vowed that the Sinaloa cartel kingpin had to be held accountable for the crimes that he committed in Mexico. In 2015, Jesús Murillo Karam, the Attorney General, said that the Mexican government would extradite Guzmán to the United States in 300 or 400 years after he served his time in Mexico.[56] This statement would later come back to haunt the Mexican government.

In July 2015, "El Chapo" Guzmán was seen walking back and forth in his cell at the Altiplano prison, located in Almoloya de Juárez. The prison video shows Guzmán removing his sandals and slipping through the shower, which connected to a tunnel that led to a construction site. President Peña Nieto, who was in France on an official state visit, asserted that the escape "represents without a doubt an affront to the Mexican state."[57] Peña Nieto assured the Mexican public that Guzmán would not escape again. The previous year, he echoed that Guzmán could not break out of prison, stating that another escape "it would be more than unfortunate, it would be unforgivable."[58] This second escape represented an international scandal for the already unpopular president. Building a tunnel was not something new for Guzmán, who had his Sinaloa cartel build dozens and dozens of tunnels along the U.S.-Mexican border to smuggle drugs. More importantly, the Mexican authorities could not control Guzmán even while behind bars.

President Peña Nieto prioritized capturing Guzmán as his escape was an international embarrassment and later extradited him to the United States. Six months after the escape of the Sinaloa cartel leader, Peña Nieto tweeted on January 6, 2016: "Mission accomplished: We have him."[59] The capture of Guzmán in Los Mochis, a town in Sinaloa, was the result of a military operation and intelligence gathering. Guzmán was planning a film about his life, and his meeting with actors Sean Penn and Kate del Castillo in October 2015 helped the government track the Sinaloa cartel kingpin.[60]

In January 2017, authorities extradited "El Chapo" Guzmán to the United States despite efforts by his attorney to block the extradition.[61] Guzmán faced ten charges in federal court. In 2019, the jury found Guzmán guilty after an 11-week trial that revealed many important allegations about the Mexican government.[62] One of the most shocking assertions that surfaced in the courtroom is that the Sinaloa cartel leader allegedly paid President Peña Nieto a $100 million bribe, highlighting the high levels of corruption present in the Mexican political system.

By the end of the Peña Nieto administration, Mexicans had very high levels of distrust in government institutions. On one hand, the 2016/2017 LAPOP data indicates that only 3.46 percent of the population answered "very satisfied" when asked their level of satisfaction with democracy. On the other hand, 49.53 percent answered "dissatisfied" and 23.97 responded "very dissatisfied." The high levels of corruption and distrust of institutions have inevitably impacted how the population feels about the political system. Moreover, the high levels of inequality and poverty despite various reform efforts have caused many Mexicans to question the efficiency of the state and whether democracy is working for them (Fig. 3.2).

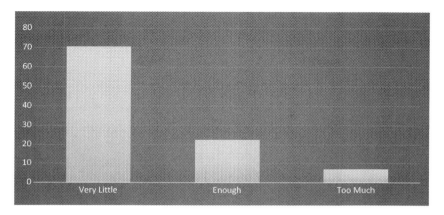

Fig. 3.2 2016/2017 Survey response to level of protection for human rights in Mexico Today. (Source: Created by author with data from LAPOP 2016/2017)

The AMLO Administration, Organized Crime, and Violence

Andrés Manuel López Obrador, known as AMLO, of the MORENA party ran for president in 2018, contending that the third time is the charm, as he had run for the presidency on two other occasions. He vowed to implement the fourth great transformation of Mexico. López Obrador focused on the need to combat the high levels of corruption hampering the country. AMLO criticized both the PRI and the PAN, often referring to them at the PRIAN. He contended that these politicians have been corrupt and have stolen from the coffers of Mexico. AMLO argued that he would not only reduce corruption, but he would end it upon assuming the presidency. He vowed not to use bodyguards and stated that he would not utilize the presidential airplane. In fact, AMLO could be seen boarding commercial airliners and flying to different campaign events. He sat coach and delivered presidential-like discourses to applauding passengers.

AMLO vowed to change the strategy regarding organized crime. He criticized Felipe Calderón for the war on drugs. He contended that Calderón turned the country into a cemetery through the militarization of the drug war. During his campaign, AMLO touted that Mexico needs "hugs not bullets."[63] He focused on addressing the underlying structural problems, including poverty and inequality as these factors contribute to the number of young people becoming involved in organized crime.

During the campaign, López Obrador discussed the possibility of providing drug traffickers with amnesty in order to reduce violence. He stated, "If it is necessary … we will talk about granting amnesty so long as the victims and their families are willing."[64] This created controversy among many analysts as they questioned the logistics of this potential policy. Moreover, there are not only two major cartels operating in Mexico, but rather there are hundreds of criminal actors. Criminal actors will want equal deals, and this could create tension about the various powerful organizations operating in the country. Granting amnesty also could foster impunity and create resentment among law-abiding citizens. The issue of credibility and trust plays an important role as ensuring that criminal actors adhere to the amnesty conditions is highly unlikely given the penchant for these groups to try to gain leverage over the government. Vanda Felbab-Brown of the Brookings Institution contends, "The proposed amnesty law for certain crimes was the most innovative and radical element of AMLO's national security strategy. Although it remains vastly underspecified it raises potentially profound, challenging, and problematic implications for the rule of law in Mexico. It entails a complex tangle of moral, legal, victims' rights, and rule of law dilemmas."[65] Ultimately, AMLO walked back his comments and said that he would propose amnesty for low-level traffickers.

López Obrador won the presidency, and the MORENA party took control of the Mexican Chamber of Deputies and the Senate. As of April 2020, MORENA holds 257 of the 500 seats, while the PAN and PRI have 78 and 46 seats, respectively. In the Mexican Senate, which has 128 Senators, MORENA has 60 senators compared to the PAN, which has 24 Senators. Other political parties, such as the PRI, hold the rest of the seats. Thus, the rejection of the PRI and the PAN not only occurred at the presidential level but also in the Mexican Congress.[66]

AMLO also inherited a country with more violence than Mexico had experienced in two decades and high levels of citizen insecurity. According to the LAPOP 2018/2019 Mexico survey, 23.12 percent of the population indicated that they felt "very insecure" when asked about perceptions of insecurity in their neighborhood. Only 13.01 percent of the population contended that they felt "very secure." Moreover, 18.97 percent of the population indicated that a family member had been a victim of extortion, while 32.93 percent answered that they had been a victim of crime in the last year.

While AMLO vowed to change the drug war strategies during his presidential campaign, he proposed the launching of a National Guard. Despite his emphasis on the need to reform the police and change the internal security strategy, López Obrador's newly minted National Guard is militarizing the internal security conflict. As history demonstrates, the militarization of the drug war has contributed to hundreds of thousands of drug-related deaths. Maureen Meyer of the Washington Office on Latin America (WOLA) echoes this point, stating: "Although the National Plan recognizes the lack of capacity and professionalization that mars Mexico's police forces, rather than focus on police reform and ending Mexico's reliance on the military as a domestic crime-fighting force, López Obrador's administration would transfer policing functions to a military-led force."[67] The fear exists that this could lead to more human rights abuses. AMLO is relying on a militarized national guard because of the higher levels of trust in the armed forces and distrust of the police. Combining the security agencies, which have different missions, goals, and budgets into one unit, creates many logistical challenges.

The National Guard and the AMLO administration came under scrutiny in October 2019, when authorities captured the son of "El Chapo" Guzmán, Ovidio Guzmán López, in Sinaloa. The capture of Guzmán and the ensuing gun battle between the National Guard and the Sinaloa cartel became viral videos on YouTube and Twitter. Mexican authorities capitulated to release Guzmán López, who was going to be extradited to the United States. The authorities maintained that they released Guzmán to save lives and stop the violence. The events that occurred in Sinaloa led to international criticism for several reasons. Alejandro Hope, a Mexican security analyst, described the event that transpired, contending: "No one could imagine such a bad Netflix show." He continued, "This combination of actually capturing the guy and then releasing him? That's new."[68] The López Obrador administration maintained that authorities stumbled upon Guzmán López, but journalists showed that such statements were a lie as this was a planned operation to arrest and extradite the son of the former Sinaloa cartel leader. Furthermore, the ability of the Sinaloa cartel to outgun and force the release of this individual signals to the public that the cartel is more powerful than the National Guard. Finally, the Sinaloa cartel now knows that it can outgun the National Guard, which will help embolden them as they seek to expand territory and control of the criminal underworld.

Opium Production and Organized Crime in Guerrero

Mexican drug traffickers have responded to the rising demand for opium and have moved into this market. In 2014, Mexico produced 42 metric tons of potential pure heroin. The potential production of heroin increased to 81 in 2016. By 2017, Mexico produced 111 metric tons of potential pure heroin. Moreover, the number of seizures of heroin at the Southwest Border of the United States has increased from 1306 kilograms in 2012 to 1854 in 2013.[69] While the number of seizures dropped between 2015 and 2016, seizures have increased in recent years. In 2018, for example, authorities seized 2321 kilograms at the Southwest Border.[70]

Guerrero has seen increases in opium cultivation and has become a battleground for the criminal underworld. Dozens of criminal groups are competing for control,[71] as the state has large fields where opium poppy is cultivated. Drug trafficking organizations bribe corrupt local officials and police officers. Traffickers also have relationships with people living in the local area. Raúl Benítez, a security expert, notes: "It is not possible to do a good job [in Guerrero]." He continues, "They are failing because of the conditions in the mountains and because drug traffickers totally control the local people and corrupt local politicians."[72] This corruption network creates perfect conditions for organized crime groups to flourish.

There are also structural and economic challenges that make poppy cultivation a lucrative enterprise. Campesino farmers earn more money growing opium than other products, despite the government's efforts. One campesino farmer, Julia Sánchez, a mother of ten children, stated: "*La goma* is the only crop that paid – nothing else sold at the market," referring to opium poppy which produces a gum that is refined into heroin. Sánchez, like other farmers living in poverty in rural Guerrero, is trying to survive. While Sánchez admits that she had heard that opium poppy is used for drugs, she participated in this endeavor to support her family; she earned around 84 pesos a day cultivating opium. She contended: "I don't know what la goma is used for – they say drugs but I don't know what that means. All I know is the only thing we know how to farm doesn't sell any more. We're desperate."[73] Having farmers substitute opium for other products, such as coffee, presents challenges as rural parts of Guerrero have limitations in terms of infrastructure. Lt. Col. Juan Jose

Orzua Padilla contends, "You get up into the mountains and look around the hillsides and there are poppy fields everywhere."[74] As seen in the Colombian case with coca, campesinos decide to cultivate this illicit product because they can earn more money. Finally, there is a security issue as traffickers can threaten campesino farmers who attempt to switch to cultivating other commodities.

How should states like Guerrero respond to the rise in opium production, a product that has fueled drug trafficking and organized crime? On February 28, 2019, Senator Manuel Añorve Baños held a day-long event in the Mexican Senate[75] where a group of experts, including academics, activists, and public officials discussed the issue of regulating opium. This represented a significant moment in Mexico as these topics had been considered taboo in past administrations. Major players in Mexican politics argued that these discussions should occur as Guerrero needs to find a solution to reducing opium production.

While regulating opium in Guerrero is an interesting conversation, there are serious challenges that exist. First, Guerrero is plagued by high levels of corruption and impunity. The institutions in the southern state are quite weak as exemplified by the case of the 43 students who were killed at the hands of the police and local gangs. Regulating any substance requires a strong state apparatus that functions effectively. Second, the fragile state apparatus in Guerrero has enabled organize crime groups to flourish. Even the Attorney General Xavier Olea maintained in 2017 that this southern state does not have the capacity to confront organized crime.[76] In summary, state weakness and fragility must be addressed before considering regulation as Guerrero has institutions that are riddled with corruption and zones within the state that are ungoverned.

Guerrero presents a major challenge for the AMLO administration. Both Guerrero and Michoacán have seen the emergence of self-defense forces who have taken the law into their own hands. The conflict between the increasing number of groups could lead to increases in violence. Moreover, criminal actors are filling the void due to the lack of state presence. The International Crisis Group echoes this point, stating: "Guerrero illustrates that López Obrador's new policies by themselves will not be enough to mitigate violent conflict. As a bellwether of crime trends in the country, the state brings alarming news, above all the continuous multiplication of local conflicts among continuously fragmenting criminal outfits, the rise of self-defence groups, the predatory turn by most criminal organisations and the depth of the authorities' complicity."[77] Solving the security crisis in Guerrero, therefore, requires addressing not only structural problems but also corruption among the police forces.

The Coronavirus and Organized Crime

The 2020 Coronavirus pandemic has impacted millions of people around the world. In Mexico, organized crime groups have attempted to increase goodwill with marginalized communities by handing out supplies for people in need. In Jalisco, the Jalisco New Generation Cartel (Cartel de Jalisco Nueva Generación—CJNG) distributed boxes of pantry products in San Luis Potosí, while the Gulf cartel has provided food for people living in The State of Tamaulipas. Los Zetas, a cartel known for its violent tactics, has provided support for residents in Veracruz. Alejandrina Gisselle, one of "El Chapo" Guzman's children, also gave elderly residents with various products. The boxes had an image of her father, the former Sinaloa cartel kingpin, and his name. The other cartels also had messages on their boxes. For example, the CJNG wrote, "On behalf of your friends from the CJNG, COVID-19 contingency support."[78]

This, however, is not the first time that cartels have handed out supplies to vulnerable populations. Instead, organized crime groups have a long history of trying to help marginalized communities. The cartels want to create support for the criminal organizations. In some zones of Mexico, such as the case of Guerrero mentioned above, the cartels are operating as de facto authorities given the inability of the state to implement the rule of law. Organized crime groups are trying to convince members of the population that they operate as security forces. Falko Ernst, a security expert, notes that in Michoacán, "To a certain extent, [the groups are] selling the notion to the population that they are the ones that provide security."[79] The pandemic will only exacerbate this problem as governments are grappling with a public health crisis. The global economy has been impacted severely, and this will have a grave effect on the millions of people living in marginalized communities in Mexico.

Combating Corruption and Impunity

Fighting organized crime, drug trafficking, and violence requires major structural reforms in Mexico. Despite reforms to the police and different institutions, corruption continues to be a serious problem. According to Transparency International's Corruptions Perceptions Index, Mexico scored 29 out of 100 in 2019, with 0 being the most corrupt and 100 being the cleanest.[80] The high levels of corruption have created distrust among the population. According to the 2018/2019 LAPOP survey, 24.38 percent of Mexicans believe that all politicians are corrupt, while 41.07 percent responded that more than half are corrupt. Only 1.43 percent responded that none are involved in corruption.

Mexico also has high impunity rates. In fact, some experts contend that impunity in Mexico is 99 percent.[81] The high levels of impunity undermine the confidence of the general public. The documented cases of collusion between organized crime and state authorities decrease the levels of confidence in the criminal justice system. Many Mexicans believe that even if they report a crime it will not be solved. The 2018/2019 LAPOP survey asked Mexicans their level of trust that the judicial system will punish the guilty. On one hand, 42.56 percent responded none, while 31.24 responded "a little." On the other hand, only 12.61 percent responded "a lot." The data, therefore, show that the population has very little trust in the judicial system. Yet trust levels in the police forces are even lower. Only 3.98 percent of Mexicans in the 2018/2019 survey responded that they have "a lot" of trust in the police. Many Mexicans do not trust the police and fear that there could be retaliation if they report a crime, given the documented cases of collusion between authorities and organized crime.

Conclusion

Drug trafficking and organized crime in Mexico have evolved over time and space. During the more than seven decades of single-party control by the PRI, the ruling party maintained intricate ties with organized crime groups through corrupt practices and strategic negotiations. The PRI's relationship with organized crime resulted in lower levels of violence. The Mexican political system was turned upside down during the transition to democracy. While this transition represented an opportunity for Mexico to reform its institutions, the country continues to be hampered by institutions laden with corruption and inefficiency.

Felipe Calderón's war on drugs led to more than 100,000 Mexicans dying from drug-related violence. The Calderón administration captured some of the major kingpins and authorities seized large quantities of drugs. The government marketed the successes of the war on drugs, but drug trafficking and organized crime flourished. The militarization of the drug war led to higher levels of violence as drug trafficking organizations fought with the government and among themselves for control of the drug trade. Despite efforts to reform the police and other institutions, corruption continued to beleaguer the state apparatus.

President Peña Nieto sought to change the security strategies in Mexico and reform institutions. While Peña Nieto altered the discourse of the war on drugs and did not market the victories, his administration continued many of his predecessors' policies. The militarization of the drug war under Peña Nieto led to more than 150,000 drug-related deaths.[82] Peña Nieto ended his presidency shrouded in scandals, including the escape of Guzmán and the 43 missing students from Guerrero. Drug trafficking, organized crime, and violence continued, and the strategies of this government created high levels of distrust in institutions across the three levels of government.

The AMLO administration faces many challenges. Reducing drug trafficking and organized crime requires addressing long-term structural issues in Mexico, such as poverty and inequality as well as reforming institutions. Despite the discourse of AMLO, he is utilizing a militarized national guard to combat drug trafficking and organized crime. This strategy could result in what has been seen in the previous administrations. AMLO must address zones in Mexican states, such as Michoacán, Guerrero, and Sinaloa, which are controlled by powerful organized crime groups that are seeking to expand their power and diversify their criminal endeavors. Unless new and innovative strategies are utilized, it is possible that Mexico witnesses increases in the power and control of organized crime groups as well as spikes in violence resulting from the militarization of the drug war.

NOTES

1. Quoted in Christopher Woody, "'La Barbie,' a US-born cartel leader and one-time partner of 'El Chapo' Guzman, sentenced to nearly 50 years in prison and a $192 million fine," *Business Insider*, June 11, 2018.
2. Christopher Woody, "'La Barbie,' a US-born cartel leader and one-time partner of 'El Chapo' Guzman, sentenced to nearly 50 years in prison and a $192 million fine."
3. Patrick Corcoran, "How Mexico's Underworld Became Violent," *InSight Crime*, March 31, 2013, https://www.insightcrime.org/news/analysis/how-mexicos-traffickers-became-violent/, accessed May 14, 2020; Patrick Corcoran, "Mexico's shifting criminal landscape: changes in gang opera-

tion and structure during the past century," *Trends in Organized Crime* 16, no. 3 (2013): pp. 306-328.
4. Patrick Corcoran, "How Mexico's Underworld Became Violent;" Peter Andreas, *Smuggler Nation: How Illicit Trade Made America* (New York, NY: Oxford University Press, 2013).
5. Patrick Corcoran, "How Mexico's Underworld Became Violent."
6. Luis Astorga and David A. Shirk, *Drug Trafficking Organizations and Counter-Drug Strategies in the U.S.-Mexican Context* (San Diego, CA: UC San Diego, 2010); Luis Alejandro Astorga Almanz, Mitología del 'narcotraficante' en México (Mexico D.F., Plaza y Valdés Editor, 1995).
7. Jorge Chabat, "Drug Trafficking in U.S.-Mexican Relations: What You See Is What You Get," in *Drug Trafficking in the Americas*, eds. Bruce M. Bagley and William O. Walker III (Coral Gables, FL: North South Center University of Miami, 1996), p. 373; William O. Walker III, *Drug Control in the Americas* (Albuquerque, NM: University of New Mexico Press, 1989).
8. Drug Enforcement Administration (DEA), "Enrique S. Camarena Special Agent," *DEA*, https://www.dea.gov/wall-of-honor/1985/03/enrique-s-camarena, accessed June 29, 2020; Gary, Feess, Robert C. Bonner, Paul Hoffman, and Manny Medrano, "The Enrique Kiki Camarena Murder and Its Aftermath," *Sw. J. Int'l L.* 23 (2017): p. 17; Shannon O'Neil, "Mexico-US Relations: What's Next?" *Americas Quarterly* 4, no. 2 (2010): pp. 68-72.
9. William Yardley, "Rubén Zuno Arce, Guilty in Drug Killing, Dies at 82," *The New York Times*, September 19, 2012.
10. Jim Newton, "Camarena's Abduction and Torture Described: Courts: Former bodyguard says ranking Mexican officials were at the house where U.S. drug agent was killed," *Los Angeles Times*, December 10, 1992.
11. Peter Watt and Roberto Zepeda, *Drug War Mexico: Politics, Neoliberalism and Violence in the New Narcoeconomy* (London, UK: Zed Books, 2012), p. 64; Stephen D. Morris and Joseph L. Klesner, "Corruption and trust: Theoretical considerations and evidence from Mexico," *Comparative Political Studies* 43, no. 10 (2010): pp. 1258-1285; Stephen D. Morris, "Drug trafficking, corruption, and violence in Mexico: mapping the linkages," *Trends in Organized Crime* 16, no. 2 (2013): pp. 195-220; Viridiana Rios, "How government coordination controlled organized crime: The case of Mexico's cocaine markets," *Journal of Conflict Resolution* 59, no. 8 (2015): pp. 1433-1454.
12. Jorge Chabat, "Drug Trafficking in U.S.-Mexican Relations: What You See Is What You Get;" Guadalupe Gonzalez, "El problema del Narcotráfico en el Contexto de la Relación entre México y Estados Unidos," *Carta de Política Exterior Mexicana* (1985): pp. 24-25; Tony Payan, "The drug war

and the US-Mexico border: The state of affairs," *South Atlantic Quarterly* 105, no. 4 (2006): pp. 863–880; Kate Doyle, "The militarization of the drug war in Mexico," *Current History* 92, no. 571 (1993): p. 83.
13. Drug Enforcement Administration (DEA), "Enrique S. Camarena Special Agent," *DEA*, https://www.dea.gov/wall-of-honor/1985/03/enrique-s-camarena, accessed May 14, 2020.
14. William Yardley, "Rubén Zuno Arce, Guilty in Drug Killing, Dies at 82."
15. Benjamin Lessing, *Making Peace in Drug Wars: Crackdowns and Cartels in Latin America* (New York, NY: Cambridge University Press, 2018), p. 215.
16. Peter Watt and Roberto Zepeda, D*rug War Mexico: Politics, Neoliberalism and Violence in the New Narcoeconomy*; Peter Andreas, *Border games: Policing the US-Mexico divide* (Ithaca, NY: Cornell University Press, 2012); Peter Andreas, "The political economy of narco-corruption in Mexico," *Current History* 97, no. 618 (1998): p. 160.
17. Louise Shelley, "Corruption and organized crime in Mexico in the post-PRI transition," *Journal of Contemporary Criminal Justice* 17, no. 3 (2001): pp. 213–231; Joseph L. Klesner, "Electoral competition and the new party system in Mexico," *Latin American Politics and Society* 47, no. 2 (2005): pp. 103–142; Ricardo Pozas-Horcasitas, "La democracia fallida: la batalla de Carlos A. Madrazo por cambiar al PRI," *Revista mexicana de sociología* 70, no. 1 (2008): pp. 47–85; Rogelio Hernández Rodríguez and Wil G. Pansters, "La democracia en México y el retorno del PRI," *Foro Internacional* (2012): pp. 755–795.
18. Christy Thornton and Adam Goodman, "How the Mexican Drug Trade Thrives on Free Trade," *The Nation*, July 15, 2014, p. 7; Peter A. Lupsha, "Drug lords and narco-corruption: The players change but the game continues," *Crime, Law and Social Change* 16, no. 1 (1991): pp. 41–58.
19. Richard Snyder and Angelica Duran-Martinez," Does illegality breed violence? Drug trafficking and state-sponsored protection rackets," *Crime, Law and Social Change* 52, no. 3 (2009): pp. 253–273; Luis Astorga and David A. Shirk, *Drug Trafficking Organizations and Counter-Drug Strategies in the U.S.-Mexican Context* (San Diego, CA: UC San Diego, 2010).
20. For more on corruption, see: Stephen D. Morris, "Corruption and Mexican political culture," *Journal of the Southwest* (2003): pp. 671–708; John J. Bailey, "Perceptions and attitudes about corruption and democracy in Mexico," *Mexican Studies/Estudios Mexicanos* 22, no. 1 (2006): pp. 57–81.
21. Luis Estrada and Alejandro Poiré, "The Mexican standoff: taught to protest, learning to lose," *Journal of Democracy* 18, no. 1 (2007): pp. 73–87; Debra Sabia and Vincent Kohler, "The 2006 Mexican Presidential Election:

Democratic Development or Democratic Debacle?" *Journal of Third World Studies* 25, no. 1 (2008): pp. 161–181.
22. For more, see: John Bailey, Pablo Parás, and Dinorah Vargas, "Army as Police? Correlates of Public Confidence in the Police, Justice System, and the Military: Mexico in Comparative Context," *Política y Gobierno* (2013): pp. 161–185; Roderic A. Camp, *Armed forces and drugs: Public perceptions and institutional challenges* (Washington, DC: Woodrow Wilson International Center for Scholars, Mexico Institute, 2010); David Pion-Berlin and Miguel Carreras, "Armed forces, police and crime-fighting in Latin America," *Journal of Politics in Latin America* 9, no. 3 (2017): pp. 3–26.
23. For more, see: Kindra Mohr, "The Merida Initiative: An Early Assessment of US-Mexico Security," *Paterson Review* 9 (2008): pp. 71–84; Stephanie Erin Brewer, "Rethinking the Mérida Initiative: Why the US must change course in its approach to Mexico's drug war," *Human Rights Brief* 16, no. 3 (2009): p. 3; Sabrina Abu-Hamdeh, "The Merida initiative: an effective way of reducing violence in Mexico?" *Pepperdine Policy Review* 4, no. 1 (2011): p. 5; Paul Ashby, "Solving the border paradox? Border security, economic integration and the mérida initiative," *Global Society* 28, no. 4 (2014): pp. 483–508.
24. Jonathan Daniel Rosen and Roberto Zepeda Martínez, "La guerra contra el narcotráfico en México: una guerra perdida," *Revista Reflexiones* 94, no. 1 (2015): pp. 153–168.
25. Direct quote from "the Merida Initiative," *U.S. Embassy & Consulates in Mexico*, https://mx.usembassy.gov/our-relationship/policy-history/the-merida-initiative/, accessed May 15, 2020.
26. Clare Ribando Seelke, *Mexico: Background and U.S. Relations* (Washington, DC, Congressional Research Service, 2020); data from Department of State and Department of Justice.
27. Clare Ribando Seelke and Kristin Finklea, *U.S.-Mexican Security Cooperation: The Mérida Initiative and Beyond* (Washington, DC: Congressional Research Service, 2017).
28. Bruce Bagley, *Drug Trafficking and Organized Crime in the Americas: Major Trends in the Twenty-First Century* (Washington, DC: Woodrow Wilson International Center for Scholars, 2012).
29. June S. Beittel, *Mexico: Organized Crime and Drug Trafficking Organizations* (Washington, DC: Congressional Research Service, 2019).
30. Patrick Corcoran, "Mexico Has 80 Drug Cartels: Attorney General," *InSight Crime*, December 20, 2012, https://www.insightcrime.org/news/analysis/mexico-has-80-drug-cartels-attorney-general/, accessed May 15, 2020.

31. June S. Beittel, *Mexico's Drug Trafficking Organizations: Source and Scope of the Violence* (Washington, DC: Congressional Research Service, 2013); Eduardo Guerrero-Gutiérrez, Security, Drugs, and Violence in Mexico: A Survey, 7th North American Forum, Washington, DC, 2011.
32. Eduardo Guerrero-Gutiérrez, *Security Drugs, and Violence in Mexico: A Survey* (Washington, DC: 7th North American Forum, 2011).
33. "Sinaloa Cartel," *InSight Crime*; for more, see: Bruce. Bagley, "Carteles de la droga: de Medellín a Sinaloa," *Criterios* 4, no. 1 (2011): pp. 233–247; Rafael Saldívar Arreola and Ignacio Rodríguez Sánchez, "La operación del cártel de Sinaloa y la transformación de la narcolengua en el noroeste de México," *Dialectologia: revista electrònica* 22 (2019): pp. 115–132; Russell Crandall, "Democracy and the Mexican Cartels," *Survival* 56, no. 3 (2014): pp. 233–244; Sam Logan, "Narco-networks in the americas," *Americas Quarterly* 4, no. 2 (2010): p. 66.
34. Quoted in "'Narconomics': How The Drug Cartels Operate Like Wal-Mart And McDonald's," *NPR*, February 15, 2016; Tom Wainwright, *Narconomics: How to Run a Drug Cartel* (New York, NY: PublicAffairs, 2016); see also: Guadalupe Correa-Cabrera, *Los Zetas Inc.: Criminal Corporations, Energy, and Civil War in Mexico* (Austin, TX: University of Texas Press, 2017).
35. "Sinaloa Cartel," *InSight Crime*; see also: Malcolm. Beith, "A broken Mexico: allegations of collusion between the Sinaloa cartel and Mexican political parties," *Small Wars & Insurgencies* 22, no. 5 (2011): pp. 787–806; Tessa Vinson, "The Sinaloa Cartel: A Study in the Dynamics of Power," *Monitor Journal* 14, no. 2 (2009): pp. 39–53.
36. Quoted in Department of Justice U.S. Attorney's Office Eastern District of New York, "Former Mexican Secretary of Public Security Arrested for Drug-Trafficking Conspiracy and Making False Statements," *Department of Justice*, December 10, 2019.
37. Department of Justice U.S. Attorney's Office Eastern District of New York, "Former Mexican Secretary of Public Security Arrested for Drug-Trafficking Conspiracy and Making False Statements."
38. Quoted in "Mexico: Over 90% of Those Killed in Drug War Are Criminals," *Latin American Herald Tribune*, http://laht.com/article.asp?ArticleI d=355578&CategoryId=10718, accessed May 15, 2020; Gobierno de los Estados Unidos Mexicanos, *6⁰ Informe de gobierno 2017–2018* (México: Gobierno de los Estados Unidos Mexicanos, 2018).
39. Kimberly Heinle, Octavio Rodríguez Ferreira, and David A. Shirk, *Drug Violence in Mexico: Data and Analysis Through 2013* (San Diego, CA: Justice in Mexico Project at University of San Diego, 2014); Justice in Mexico, *Memoria* dataset.

40. For more, see: Julien Mercille, "Violent narco-cartels or US hegemony? The political economy of the 'war on drugs' in Mexico," *Third World Quarterly* 32, no. 9 (2011): pp. 1637–1653; Howard Campbell and Tobin Hansen, "Is Narco-Violence in Mexico Terrorism?" *Bulletin of Latin American Research* 33, no. 2 (2014): pp. 158–173; Peter Reuter, "Systemic violence in drug markets," *Crime, Law and Social Change* 52, no. 3 (2009): pp. 275–284; David Shirk and Joel Wallman, "Understanding Mexico's drug violence," *Journal of Conflict Resolution* 59, no. 8 (2015): pp. 1348–1376; Paul Gootenberg, "Blowback: the Mexican drug crisis," *NACLA Report on the Americas* 43, no. 6 (2010): pp. 7–12.

41. For more, see: Jonathan D. Rosen and Roberto Zepeda, *Organized Crime, Drug Trafficking, and Violence in Mexico: The Transition from Felipe Calderón to Enrique Peña Nieto* (Lanham, MD: Lexington Books, 2016).

42. Victoria Dittmar, "The Mexico Crime Bosses Peña Nieto's Government Toppled," *InSight Crime*, September 24, 2018, https://www.insightcrime.org/news/analysis/mexico-crime-bosses-pena-nietos-government-toppled/, accessed May 15, 2020.

43. Alberto Lozano-Vázquez and Jorge Rebolledo Flores, "In Search of the Mérida Initiative: From Antecedents to Practical Results," *Drug Trafficking, Organized Crime, and Violence in the Americas Today*, eds. Bruce M. Bagley and Jonathan D. Rosen (Gainesville, FL: University Press of Florida, 2015): pp. 239–256.

44. Anna Grace, "10 Years of the Mérida Initiative: Violence and Corruption," *InSight Crime*, December 26, 2018, https://www.insightcrime.org/news/analysis/merida-initiative-failings-violence-corruption/, accessed May 15, 2020, p. 3.

45. Isaí T. Lara Bermúdez, "Hubo más ejecuciones con Enrique Peña Nieto que con Felipe Calderón," *Proceso*, December 5, 2018.

46. Quoted in Kirk Semple, "Missing Mexican Students Suffered a Night of 'Terror,' Investigators Say," *The New York Times*, April 24, 2016.

47. "Guerreros Unidos," *InSight Crime*, April 8, 2015, https://www.insightcrime.org/mexico-organized-crime-news/guerreros-unidos-mexico/, accessed May 20, 2020.

48. Interview at National Public Radio (NPR), "What Happened To Mexico's Missing 43 Students In 'A Massacre In Mexico,'" *NPR*, October 21, 2018.

49. Randal C. Archibold, "Investigators in Mexico Detain Mayor and His Wife Over Missing Students," *The New York Times*, November 4, 2014.

50. Maureen Meyer and Gina Hinojosa, "Five Years On, Still No Justice for Mexico's 43 Disappeared Ayotzinapa Students," *Washington Office on Latin America*, September 24, 2019, https://www.wola.org/analysis/five-year-anniversary-ayotzinapa-mexico/, accessed May 20, 2020; Washington Office on Latin America (WOLA), "How a New Report

Challenges Mexico's 'Official Version' of the Case of 43 Disappeared Students," *WOLA*, September 9, 2015, https://www.wola.org/analysis/how-a-new-report-challenges-mexicos-official-version-of-the-case-of-43-disappeared-students/, accessed May 20, 2020.
51. Quoted in Reuters, "U.N. accuses Mexico of torture, cover-up in case of 43 missing students," *Reuters*, March 15, 2018.
52. Maureen Meyer and Gina Hinojosa, "Five Years On, Still No Justice for Mexico's 43 Disappeared Ayotzinapa Students."
53. Quoted in Marina Franco, "Five Years Ago, 43 Students Vanished. The Mystery, and the Pain, Remain," *The New York Times*, Sept. 26, 2019.
54. Marina Franco, "Five Years Ago, 43 Students Vanished. The Mystery, and the Pain, Remain."
55. Randal C. Archibold and Ginger Thompson, "El Chapo, Most-Wanted Drug Lord, Is Captured in Mexico," *The New York Times*, February 22, 2014.
56. Alan Feuer, "El Chapo, Accused Drug Lord, Questions Legality of His Extradition From Mexico," *The New York Times*, August 3, 2017.
57. Alan Feuer, "El Chapo, Accused Drug Lord, Questions Legality of His Extradition From Mexico," *The New York Times*, July 12, 2015.
58. Alan Feuer, "El Chapo, Accused Drug Lord, Questions Legality of His Extradition From Mexico."
59. Azam Ahmed, "El Chapo, Escaped Mexican Drug Lord, Is Recaptured in Gun Battle," *The New York Times*. January 8, 2016.
60. Azam Ahmed, "El Chapo, Escaped Mexican Drug Lord, Is Recaptured in Gun Battle;" Mike LaSusa and Parker Asmann, "Did Sean Penn's Meeting With El Chapo Help Authorities Track Down the Kingpin?" *InSight Crime*, November 8, 2017.
61. Azam Ahmed, "El Chapo, Mexican Drug Kingpin, Is Extradited to U.S.," *The New York Times*, January 19, 2017.
62. Emily Palmer and Alan Feuer, "El Chapo Trial: The 11 Biggest Revelations From the Case," *The New York Times*, February 3, 2019.
63. José Reyez, "Calderón convirtió al país en un cementerio: AMLO," Contralinea, August 29, 2019; Humberto Beck, Carlos Bravo Regidor, and Patrick Iber, "Year One of AMLO's Mexico," *Dissent* 67, no. 1 (2020): pp. 109–118.
64. Quoted in David Agren, "Fury as Mexico presidential candidate pitches amnesty for drug cartel kingpins," *The Guardian*, December 4, 2017.
65. Vanda Felbab-Brown, "Should Mexico revive the idea of amnesty for criminals," *Brookings*, March 2, 2020, https://www.brookings.edu/blog/order-from-chaos/2020/03/02/should-mexico-revive-the-idea-of-amnesty-for-criminals/, accessed May 20, 2020, p. 2.

66. Clare Ribando Seelke, *Mexico: Background and U.S. Relations* (Washington, DC: Congressional Research Service, 2020); data from Mexican Chamber of Deputies, Mexican Senate.
67. Maureen Meyer, "Mexico's Proposed National Guard Would Solidify the Militarization of Public Security," *Washington Office on Latin America*, January 10, 2019, https://www.wola.org/analysis/mexico-national-guard-military-abuses/, accessed May 20, 2020, p. 1.
68. Quoted in Azam Ahmed, "The Stunning Escape of El Chapo's Son: It's Like 'a Bad Netflix Show,'" *The New York Times*, October 18, 2019.
69. Drug Enforcement Administration (DEA), 2019: *National Drug Threat Assessment* (Springfield, VA: DEA, 2019).
70. For more, see: Drug Enforcement Administration (DEA), 2019: *National Drug Threat Assessment* (Springfield, VA: DEA, 2019).
71. James Fredrick, "On The Hunt For Poppies In Mexico—America's Biggest Heroin Supplier," *NPR*, January 14, 2018.
72. Quoted in James Fredrick, "On The Hunt For Poppies In Mexico—America's Biggest Heroin Supplier."
73. Quoted in The Guardian, "US fentanyl crisis could end opium era in Mexico: 'the only crop that paid,'" *The Guardian*, May 2, 2019.
74. Quoted in James Fredrick, "On The Hunt For Poppies In Mexico—America's Biggest Heroin Supplier."
75. I had the honor of participating in this event.
76. Deborah Bonello, "Guerrero, Mexico Can't Confront Organized Crime: State Attorney General," *InSight Crime*, March 27, 2017, https://www.insightcrime.org/news/brief/guerreromexico-cant-confront-organized-crime-state-attorney-general/, accessed May 23, 2020, p. 1.
77. International Crisis Group, Mexico's Everyday War: Guerrero and the Trials of Peace (Brussels: International Crisis Group, 2020), p. 31.
78. Victoria Dittmar, "Mexico Cartels Hand Out Food Amid Coronavirus Pandemic," *InSight Crime*, April 28, 2020, https://www.insightcrime.org/news/analysis/mexico-cartels-hand-out-food-coronavirus-pandemic/, accessed May 23, 2020; "CJNG reparte despensas para ayudar a familias en tiempos del coronavirus," *La Opinión*, April 15, 2020; Juan Alberto Cedillo, "El Cartel del Golfo reparte despensas en Tamaulipas por covid-19," *Proceso*, April 6, 2020.
79. Quoted in Victoria Dittmar, "Mexico Cartels Hand Out Food Amid Coronavirus Pandemic."
80. See "Corruption Perceptions Index," *Transparency International*, https://www.transparency.org/en/countries/mexico, accessed July 16, 2020.
81. James Bargent, "Mexico Impunity Levels Reach 99%: Study," *InSight Crime*, February 4, 2016, https://www.insightcrime.org/news/brief/

mexico-impunity-levels-reach-99-study/, accessed May 25, 2020; Juan Antonio Le Clercq Ortega and Gerardo Rodríguez Sánchez Lara, *Global Impunity Index Mexico 2016* (Puebla, MX: Universidad de las Américas Puebla, 2016).

82. For more, see: Isaí T. Lara Bermúdez, "Hubo más ejecuciones con Enrique Peña Nieto que con Felipe Calderón," *Proceso*, December 5, 2018.

CHAPTER 4

Addiction, Fentanyl, and the Border

Abstract This chapter focuses on the issue of drug addiction as well as the trafficking of drugs through Mexico en route to the United States. It begins with an examination of OxyContin and the Sackler family. It focuses on the role that marketing played in the opioid crisis in the United States. This chapter also provides stories of addiction, focusing on the real-world impact that the opioid epidemic has had on people. It then turns to the case of fentanyl and Philadelphia, analyzing not only drug trafficking but also alternative policies, such as safe injection sites. Finally, it explains how drugs are trafficked through the border from Mexico.

Keywords Fentanyl • Addiction • Philadelphia • Laboratories • Opioid epidemic • Southern border

This chapter examines addiction from several angles as the opioid epidemic costs the U.S. government $78.5 billion per year.[1] It explores the role of pharmaceutical companies in producing and marketing opioids. Critics contend that these companies downplayed the impacts of opioids and pills prescribed by medical providers to help patients decrease their pain levels.[2] This chapter also looks at fentanyl, its derivatives, and the impact that this drug has had on the United States. It focuses on the case study of Philadelphia, which has been trying new strategies, including safe injection sites, to combat opioid overdoses. This chapter then examines where fentanyl comes from and the issue of border security. The Donald Trump administration touted a wall with Mexico as the solution to combating drug trafficking and organized crime. The concluding section examines the challenges of stopping the flow of drugs, given the interconnectedness between countries in today's globalized world.

OxyContin, Marketing, and Addiction

There are several underlying variables that have contributed to the opioid epidemic in the United States. One of the principal factors has been that some doctors have overprescribed opioids to patients. The Sackler family are the owners of Purdue Pharma, which is the company that released OxyContin in 1995. The Sackler family's enterprise and pharmaceutical revolution began with three brothers, Raymond, Mortimer, and Arthur. Arthur died in 1987, while the other two brothers died in 2010 and 2017.[3] Arthur became a marketing guru as he contended that advertising required selling not only to the patient but also to the doctors treating these individuals. While Arthur became a marketing and advertising specialist, critics maintain that he utilized deceptive practices. In 1952, the three brothers, all of whom were trained as psychiatrists, purchased Purdue Frederick, a company operating out of New York City. In the 1960s, Arthur had tremendous financial success selling tranquilizers such as Valium, although he led such marketing campaigns through another organization, not Purdue Frederick.[4]

After his death in 1987, Arthur's estate sold more than $22 million in stock options to his two brothers, who controlled Purdue. Raymond and Mortimer as well as Richard, the son of Raymond, increased the family's fortune through the aggressive promotion of OxyContin, which is produced by Purdue Pharma. This company remains a privately owned company. The families of Raymond and Mortimer own 100 percent of Purdue Pharma[5] and made up most of the company's board.[6] The key ingredient in this drug is oxycodone, which is known as the "chemical cousin" of heroin. Critics contend that the Sackler family undersold the potential dangers of this new miracle drug. Purdue Pharma excelled at marketing the drug and tried to convince doctors of the benefits of this miracle product.

Experts maintain that Purdue Pharma misled providers and focused on the benefits of the drug. The company also countered the narrative about the dangers of this drug. The company funded various research studies and sponsored doctors to discuss the advantages of this new miracle drug. Brandeis University's Andrew Kolodny contends, "If you look at the prescribing trends for all the different opioids, it's in 1996 that prescribing really takes off." He continues, "It's not a coincidence. That was the year Purdue launched a multifaceted campaign that misinformed the medical community about the risks."[7] This marketing campaign led to increases in the number of drugs being prescribed and made the Sackler family billionaires.[8]

Doctors who overprescribed this drug are responsible for opioid addiction crises that America faces today. The cases of excessive prescribing and pill mills[9] are exemplified by Tug Valley, a small-scale pharmacy that opened in 2006 and provided millions of pills to a town in West Virginia that had just 3000 people living in this area. Samuel R Ballengee owned these pharmacies and began increasing the number of orders for opioids to this small town. Some law enforcement officials contended that this enterprise constituted a drug cartel. One West Virginia state police officer, Sergeant Mike Smith, stated: "Let's call this whole thing what it is. It's pretty much a cartel. A drug trafficking organisation," He continued: "Then right in the middle of this drug trafficking organisation, you have a little pharmacy that pops up and everybody's OK with it. I'm sitting here looking at this. It's hard to believe that was allowed."[10] The drug distributors provided three pharmacies in this poverty-stricken town with more than 30 million opioids, fueling the addiction rates devastating West Virginia. In 2017, for example, West Virginia had 833 deaths from drug overdoses, which is equivalent to a rate of 49.6 per 100,000 inhabitants. In 2018, West Virginia recorded 702 drug-related deaths—a rate of 42.4 per 100,000 people.[11]

Authorities arrested Ballengee as well as Anthony Rattini, who served as the president of Miami-Luken, the company that supplied Ballengee's operations. Authorities alleged that Ratitini supplied more than 200 pharmacies in Tennessee, Indiana, Ohio, and West Virginia with opioids.[12] The opioid distribution helped the Miami-Luken company earn more than $173 million in sales each year. The pharmacy operated by Ballengee obtained more than 120,000 pills from Miami-Luken in one month alone, demonstrating the massive quantity of pills being sent to this small West Virginia town—a town which had many more pills than people. Miami-Luken also provided the pharmacy owned by Ballengee with more than six million hydrocodone pills between 2008 and 2014.[13]

There have been more cases of doctors who have abused their medical credentials by running "pill-mills," or places where doctors simply push pills and make exorbitant amounts of money.[14] In February 2019, the U.S. Attorney's Office of the Eastern District of Pennsylvania charged 14 people for operating "pill mills" through Advanced Urgent Care (AUC). Mehdi Nikparvar-Fard, the owner of AUC, provided "pain management" services for $80 to $140. This service consisted of physicians flooding the streets with opioids as doctors from AUC distributed at least 3678 illegal prescriptions. U.S. Attorney William M. McSwain states, "As alleged in these indictments, thousands of illegally prescribed pills flooded our streets because of the conduct of these defendants. My Office will continue to do its part to enforce our nation's drug laws and hold physicians, physician's assistants, and their agents accountable. As these indictments show, medical professionals who violate their oaths and exploit their patients' addictions to make an easy buck will be prosecuted to the fullest extent of the law."[15] The defendants, in this case, pushed these addictive pills in exchange for cash and violated their professional responsibilities as healthcare providers. According to the Special Agent in charge of the Drug Enforcement Administration's Philadelphia Field Division, Jonathan A. Wilson, "The defendants arrested in this case are accused of setting up and operating a scheme in which the defendants sold opioid prescriptions to individuals without any legitimate medical need or purpose in exchange for cash. The defendants issued 3,678 prescriptions which amounted to hundreds of thousands of pills being used by addicted individuals."[16]

The federal government has continued to prosecute healthcare professionals who have violated the ethical standards and contributed to the opioid epidemic. Authorities, for example, arrested Osasuyi Kenneth Idumwonyi, and the courts later sentenced him to more than 100 months in federal prison in June 2019. Idumwonyi and his nurse practitioner, Julie Ann DeMille, operated a pill mill that wrote thousands of prescriptions for opioids in Portland, Oregon. This, however, was not the first time that this medical professional ran such operations. In 2009, he operated clinics in Houston, Texas, that illegally prescribed opioids. Idumwonyi required patients to give him kickbacks—in the form of pills—for the right to return to his clinic, where he continued to overprescribe opioids. DeMille wrote more than 1900 prescriptions, nearly 97 percent of them for opioids. For her involvement in this operation, the courts sentenced DeMille to four years in federal prison.[17]

People sometimes turn to heroin and other illicit drugs when doctors stop writing them prescriptions for opioids. The consequence of overprescribing, which has fueled addiction, is that 200,000 people have died from opioids in the United States since 1999. In 2010, the United States recorded 38,329 overdoses, but this number increased to 70,237 in 2017.[18] In 2018, more than 67,000 people died from a drug overdose in the United States.[19] Today, it is more likely that someone will die from a drug overdose than a car accident. In 2017, the odds of dying in a car crash were 1 and 103 compared to 1 and 96 for an opioid overdose. On average, 130 Americans died every day from an opioid overdose, revealing the crisis that the United States currently is facing.[20]

Some states have been hit especially hard. In 2017, Ohio had 5111 deaths, which is a death rate of 46.3 per 100,000 people, while Pennsylvania had 5388—a rate of 44.3 per 100,000 inhabitants. Kentucky, New Hampshire, and Delaware had rates of 37.2, 37, and 37, respectively, while New Jersey, Connecticut, Rhode Island, Massachusetts, Maine, and Maryland had rates between 30 and 36.3 per 100,000 inhabitants (Figs. 4.1 and 4.2).[21]

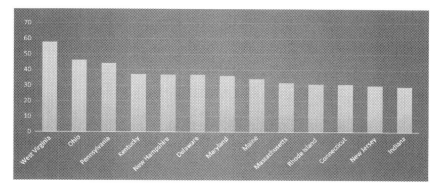

Fig. 4.1 2017 Age-adjusted death rate per 100,000. (Source: Created by author with data from 2017 Drug Overdose Death Rates, Center for Disease Control and Prevention)

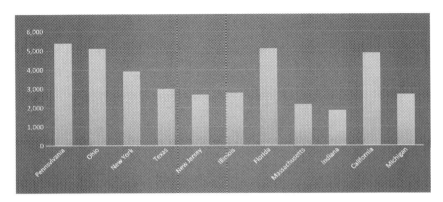

Fig. 4.2 Number of deaths from drug overdose (2017). (Source: Created by author with data from 2017 Number of Drug Overdose Deaths, Center for Disease Control and Prevention)

STORIES OF ADDICTION

The opioid epidemic has had countless impacts on families throughout the United States. Journalistic accounts tell some of the stories of those impacted by the opioid crisis. For example, the class of 2000 of Minford, Ohio, was described by Dan Levin as a group of students that could have done anything. However, the opioid epidemic derailed many of these individual's lives. Ashley Moore, a student who belonged to the honors society, recounted how the opioid epidemic has impacted her life: "OxyContin just started showing up at parties around junior year. People wanted to try it. It was fun. It got to where kids were doing it in the parking lot before school. By senior year it was so common."[22] Some of her classmates, such as Johnathan Whitt, became addicted to painkillers. Whitt, who has been arrested on at least ten occasions, started using the readily available pills. He described his struggles with opioids, contending: "I started seeing a lot of pills around 15 years old and I told myself I was never going to do them. But kids were selling Oxys at school for $3 a pill. By the time I was 19, I was looking in every medicine cabinet and bathroom. All of my close friends, we all turned into drug addicts."[23]

Addiction is not only physically destructive, but it has a severe financial impact on users. Jake Bradshaw, another member of the class of 2000, played soccer and baseball while in high school. He started using opioids and dabbled in cocaine and heroin, which cost him at one point an estimated $400 per day. He maintains that drug addiction severely impacted his life: "The consequences started happening in college. By this point I was physically dependent on OxyContin, but it was very easy to tell myself, 'I don't do crack, I don't shoot up.' That messed me up for a really long time."[24] This individual, like many others suffering from addiction, was arrested and went to rehabilitation facilities on multiple occasions.

In the section below, several people who have suffered from opioid addiction talk about addiction and its challenges:

> My first several months on opiates saw me as productive and social and ambitious as I'd ever been. It felt as though I had a secret superpower, a key to success that made me all but invincible. But the diminishing returns were always threatening. The effects would wear off quicker, the dose I would need increased. And before long, the upkeep of my back-pocket superpower took the top spot on my priority list.—Stephen DePasque, 35, Clifton Heights, Pennsylvania.

> I didn't plan on becoming addicted, but somewhere along the way I became dependent, and it seemed impossible to quit. After quitting, there's a long and grueling mental addiction to battle as well. This is the hard part. Heroin is but a symptom of a bigger problem. Until I was able to understand why I used and change myself, I could never stop using.—Erin Castle, 27, West Milton, Ohio

> At age 26, my little brother and I found our big brother dead on the floor from an accidental fentanyl overdose. I actually took the rest of his dope and did it in a McDonald's bathroom while the coroner was loading him into a van. As sick and twisted as that is. But that's addiction. Sick and twisted. It's like being in an endless tunnel. You can see the light at the end, but you never feel like you'll reach it.—Heather Hudson, 27, St. Louis, Missouri.[25]

These stories highlight the trauma of addiction and how potent opioids are.

While opioid overdoses represent a public health crisis, there are many success stories of people who have recovered from their addictions.[26] Katherine, a 29-year-old from Philadelphia, describes her philosophy on recovery, stating: "Recovery is not an exact science, or a recipe that can be applied to different people in different ways. But many of us do recover. I wish I knew the answer to this current crisis. All I can do is keep my hand open and available to the next person who may need help."[27] Recovery is a long process and people must overcome cravings and factors, including stress that can lead them back to drug consumption.

Patrick McElwaine, a professor of counseling psychology in Philadelphia, focuses on helping people overcome addiction and decreasing the stigma associated with labels. Professor McElwaine, who has been in recovery for years, stresses that people must overcome the underlying traumas that contribute to drug consumption. He frequently speaks to audiences about his personal battles with addiction. He explains how he used drugs and alcohol to cope with low self-esteem as well as the trauma from losing his father, who died from drowning when McElwaine was nine years old while his family was on vacation. The toxicology report indicated that his father had approximately six beers in his system. Professor McElwaine turned to alcohol and later started using pills, which were easier to hide from his wife and family as one can smell alcohol on someone's breath.[28] His story and professional work serve as an example for many people struggling to overcome the stigma associated with addiction.

THE FENTANYL FURY: THE CASE OF PHILADELPHIA

Fentanyl is a synthetic drug that has emerged on the scene and has destroyed many lives.[29] This synthetic opioid is between 80 and 100 times more powerful than drugs like morphine. Fentanyl is used in surgeries and is also designed to help cancer patients manage their pain levels. This drug is abused through a variety of delivery mechanisms, including taking pills, smoking it, and injecting it.[30] There are various fentanyl analogs like carfentanil, furanylfentanyl, and acetylfentanyl. Experts estimate that carfentanil is around 100 times more powerful than fentanyl.[31] Carfentanil is so potent that it is used as a tranquilizer for large animals like rhinos.[32]

The City of Philadelphia has been hit hard by Fentanyl and other opioids as more than 3000 people died over the past three years.[33] Public health officials have also confirmed carfentanil-related death cases in this city. The epicenter of drug sales and usage is in Kensington, which is a microcosm of the opioid crisis. Kensington has been described as the "Walmart of heroin" as people from around the United States have come to this neighborhood, one which is inflicted with drugs, crime, and violence, to buy heroin. Kensington is not far from Interstate-95, which connects New York to Miami. Mark, a wounded Iraq war veteran who turned to heroin to cope with a pain pill addiction, purchased drugs laced with fentanyl in Kensington. According to Mark, "It was like the alien in the movie was going to pop out of my chest, things I've never experienced going through detox before."[34] The potent substance only trapped Mark in this area as he sought drugs to meet his cravings. "I knew then that I wasn't going to leave," Mark recounted.[35]

The large quantity of drugs in Kensington has led to vast numbers of people living under bridges and on the street. One man named George stated: "People think we are having fun down here. Are you insane? I live under a bridge." He maintained that Kensington made it easier to be homeless, given the number of people living here and the pervasiveness of drugs. According to George, "You get help up here. You get food. Everything I have I was given from somebody. The drugs are here — they are closer and cheaper."[36] Another drug user, a 30-year-old named Krista who started using drugs to cope with the trauma following a sexual assault in college, felt an attraction pulling her back toward Kensington. She stated: "If I'm a little further away, I have this nervous feeling that I need to come back to Kensington." Krista contended: "It's like a big dysfunctional family. I guess this is the one place I belong."[37] The easy access to drugs and large community of people addicted to opioids has remained a constant in this downtrodden neighborhood, representing a public health crisis for the city.

Law enforcement authorities have attempted to combat drug trafficking in Kensington, and other areas in Philadelphia. Gang activity has increased over time. The Philadelphia Police Department, for instance, identified 169 gangs in the city and the immediate surrounding suburbs between 2009 and 2013. The police indicate that the number of gangs increased by 76 percent over four years. Federal authorities have noted that Dominican criminal groups operate the distribution of prescription drugs and cocaine in certain sections of Philadelphia. Authorities highlight that larger organized crime groups from Mexico have utilized Philadelphia as a hub for distributing drugs given its population, access to water, and location as it is close to several major cities, including New York and Washington, D.C.[38]

Gang and drug activity as well as access to guns have contributed to violence in the city. Philadelphia has seen a rise in the number of homicides since 2013, when it recorded 246. The city had 315 homicides in 2017 and 356 in 2019.[39] In June 2019, Philadelphia had a very violent weekend, with 28 victims and five deaths as a result of 19 shootings.[40] In

October 2019, two shootings occurred in one weekend that left an 11-month-old child in critical condition and killed a two-year-old girl. Mayor Jim Kenney stated: "You feel like you're making progress in the city and then this weekend happens."[41] Maria D. Quiñones-Sánchez, a councilwoman who represents the districts where the tragic events occurred, maintained that the shootings likely were drug-related. She asserted: "There are 500 people in active addiction that are also homeless in the area." She continued, "What that creates is an open-air drug market, with an active customer base. There is deep poverty and not enough restorative investment in the people trapped in it."[42] These events have fueled violence and have led citizens to call for Philadelphia officials to "clean up" the streets.

There have been a series of arrests and prison sentences of people operating drug trafficking networks in Kensington as authorities have sought to combat the seemingly endless flow of drugs impacting this impoverished area in North Philadelphia. In 2012, for example, Judge Juan R. Sanchez sentenced Alexander Rivera to a life sentence in prison along with another 60 months. Rivera was a known drug leader in North Philadelphia who operated the Alexander Rivera Narcotics Distribution Organization ("ARDO") drug operation in Kensington. Rivera, known as "Reds" for his red hair and beard, controlled several blocks in Kensington and distributed heroin, PCP, cocaine, and crack. Rivera ordered homicides on people who crossed him. In September 2006, Rivera shot an innocent person in the area while engaged in a gunfight.[43] Rivera profited off the addiction of people living in Philadelphia. The Assistant U.S. Attorney claimed that Rivera sold around $18,000 of crack cocaine between 2006 and 2010. Rivera's narcotics business became a family affair, as he stored drugs in his garage. The courts also convicted his wife Ileana Vidal for drug-related offenses.[44]

Another case highlighting the powerful drug trade in Philadelphia is that of Juan Jarmon. In November 2019, the courts sentenced Jarmon to 30 years in prison for a litany of crimes that he committed while leading a gang in North Philadelphia. He ran his drug trade out of the public housing apartments in North Philadelphia. Jarmon's operations included a variety of criminal activities from cooking and distributing crack cocaine to even providing protection for other individuals involved in the drug trade. U.S. Attorney McSwain stated, "Here, Jarmon and his co-defendants used firearms, robbed rival drug dealers, and used intimidation, threats, and violence to further their 'business' of moving poison on our streets.

Philadelphia residents can rest easier knowing that Jarmon is behind bars and his drug gang has been destroyed."[45] Authorities contended that Jarmon utilized various violent tactics to control the drug business and intimidate the residents living within the public housing units.

THE NATION'S FIRST SAFE INJECTION SITE IN PHILADELPHIA

In addition to combating the dealers operating in Philadelphia, the city has been in court battles over safe injection sites. In February 2020, a court ruling indicated that a non-profit organization known as Safehouse would not be in violation of federal laws for operating a safe injection site, which provides drug users a supervised location to use drugs.[46] The goal of the safe injection site is to provide a safe facility for drug users to prevent overdoses from occurring in locations where medical personnel are not available. Safehouse notes that the following professionals will render services: "Medically trained professionals, certified peer specialists, recovery specialists, social workers, and case managers specializing in overdose prevention and harm reduction will provide Safehouse services."[47] This safe injection site does not provide the users with drugs, but rather it seeks to save lives as someone using drugs in their home or an abandoned drug house could die from an overdose.

Critics of safe injection sites argue that they promote drug usage. The U.S. Attorney for the Eastern District of Pennsylvania has publicly criticized this safe injection site and contended that he would appeal the judge's ruling. According to McSwain, "What Safehouse proposes is a radical experiment that would invite thousands of people onto its property for the purpose of injecting illegal drugs."[48] It is alleged that safe houses are violating the Controlled Substance Act, known as the "crack house statute,"[49] which outlaws owning property where illegal drugs are being consumed. Supporters of safe injection sites believe that this is a misinterpretation of the law and assert that the U.S. Congress did not intend for the law to apply to public health facilities trying to help people addicted to drugs.[50] Proponents of safe injection sites in Philadelphia contend that McSwain is trying to prevent actions designed to save lives. Safehouse indicates that participants will receive information about rehabilitation at multiple points. Professionals also will conduct a behavioral and physical health assessment of each person.[51]

The city of Philadelphia, particularly in places like Kensington, has been one of the epicenters of the opioid epidemic, and this would be the first safe injection site in the United States. More than 3000 people died from the opioid crisis in a three-year period, demonstrating the public health crisis that the city currently faces. Over the past ten years, the number of deaths of the homeless population living in the city has increased by threefold.[52] Advocates of safe injection sites like Safehouse argue that these sites are trying to help people stop using drugs and take whatever steps are necessary to prevent deaths.[53] Yet McSwain and other critics maintain that the research about the effects of safe injection sites is rather limited.[54]

The U.S. Southern Border and Drug Flows: The Supply of Fentanyl

Some policymakers have focused on combating the supply of fentanyl and the need to increase border security. China is a major supplier of fentanyl precursors because of the loose regulations of chemicals from laboratories.[55] Mexican transnational organized crime groups are customers of the chemical precursors.[56] In addition, 97 percent of Fentanyl that U.S. authorities have seized being shipped via international mail is from China. The Chinese government has vowed to strengthen restrictions to combat the sale of the chemical precursors, which has caused criminal organizations in Mexico to attempt to diversify the sources of this key ingredient used to make fentanyl.[57]

At the Group of 20 summit in Buenos Aires, Argentina, in 2018, both the U.S. and Chinese presidents met. President Xi Jinping vowed to label fentanyl as a controlled substance and do more to stop the supply. China has stepped up its enforcement and has combated the fentanyl trade. The deputy director of the country's National Narcotics Control Commission stated: "China's control over fentanyl substances is becoming stricter and stricter." The government has convicted people for smuggling fentanyl.[58] In November 2019, for example, a Chinese court sentenced Liu Yong to death for operating a clandestine system of labs that produced and shipped fentanyl to the United States.[59]

In Mexico, precursors are processed into fentanyl and transported by sea, air, and land to the U.S. border. Experts note that around 75 percent of fake pills and fentanyl crossed the border at the Tijuana-San Diego checkpoint through a variety of mechanisms, including drug "mules," container trucks, and passenger cars. As will be discussed in more detail below, the sheer number of cars that cross through the border every day, month, and year make it very difficult to stop the flow of drugs.[60]

The United States has seen increases in Fentanyl seizures nationwide from 595 pounds in FY2016 to 2545 in FY2019. The monthly drug seizures in 2019 have remained relatively stable with some ebbs and flows. In October, nationwide field offices seized 248 pounds of Fentanyl. The number of seizures declined to 94 pounds in January but increased to 216 pounds in March (Fig. 4.3).[61]

President Donald Trump campaigned on the need to implement the rule of law and improve border security. He offended many people around the world when he made derogatory comments about people coming from Mexico, a large country with more than 120 million people. Trump vowed to build a wall between Mexico and the United States to stop not only the illegal immigration but the flow of drugs. During the 2016 campaign, Trump led "build that wall" chants at his rallies. Moreover, he promised that the Mexican government will pay for the wall. He would often ask his supporters to respond to Mexico when he would yell who is

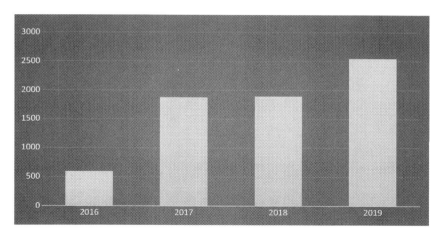

Fig. 4.3 Nationwide drug seizures of fentanyl between FY 2016-FY 2020 (in pounds). (Source: Created by author with data from "CBP Enforcement Statistics Fiscal Year 2020," U.S. Customs and Border Protection)

going to pay for the wall. Past and former Mexican presidents responded that Mexico would not pay for the wall.[62]

Critics contend that the wall is too costly. The U.S. government shares a 2000-mile border with Mexico. Moreover, there is already 650 miles of fencing and border wall that the Bush and Obama administrations constructed. Since assuming office, the Trump administration vowed to construct 576 miles of what it referred to as a new "border wall system." This cost $20 million per mile, totaling $11 billion. The Trump administration allocated $15 billion in resources for the construction of the remainder of the border wall, a figure almost double the amount of support of the initial Covid-19 emergency response act.[63] This wall, therefore, will be the most expensive border wall on the planet.[64]

During a 2020 rally in Milwaukee, Trump asserted: "You're going to have a wall like no other. It's going to be a powerful, terrific wall." He continued, "A very big and very powerful border wall is going up at a record speed, and we are fully financed now, isn't that nice?"[65] The higher price tag for the wall is due not only to the labor and supply costs but also to the terrain between Mexico and the United States. Critics note that the Army Corps of Engineers detonated controlled blasts near Monument Hill, a sacred heritage site in Arizona for Native Americans. Moreover, the workers bulldozed and detonated explosives to work on building the wall near another national monument near Tucson, Arizona, leading to questions about the environmental damages that are being causes to important historic locations along the southwest border. Laiken Jordahl, an environmental activist, expressed his discontent with the construction of the border wall, stating: "[Chad] Wolf, [the Secretary of Homeland Security,] is responsible for ramming border walls into our communities, bulldozing our state's beloved saguaro cactuses and demolishing indigenous sacred sites."[66]

Combating the flow of drugs and goods crossing the southern border is an arduous task. Thousands of cars legally cross the U.S.-Mexican border every day for a variety of purposes, including commerce. The Bureau of Transportation Statistics records the number of border crossings. The data reflect the number of pedestrians, passengers, containers, and vehicles entering the United States.[67] In 2019, San Ysidro, California, for instance, recorded more than 14.9 million crossings. Moreover, El Paso Texas, which borders Ciudad Juárez, recorded more than 11.3 million crossings in 2019, followed by Otay Mesa, California with more than 7.5 million.[68] In Brownsville, Texas, 523,214 personal vehicles crossed the border in

March 2020, along with 176,254 pedestrians, 419 buses, and 2572 bus passengers.[69] Thus, the data indicate that the number of legal crossings is in the millions per year. This number will remain high with or without a wall as cars and buses can drive through checkpoints.

Conclusion

The United States is facing an opioid epidemic. Today, it is more likely that someone will die of an opioid overdose than in a car accident. The opioid epidemic has impacted people from all walks of life and does not discriminate based on age, sex, or socioeconomic class. Pharmaceutical companies have played a major role in the crisis by marketing highly addictive pain pills. People who are unable to get a prescription from a doctor turned to other drugs on the streets to feed their addictions. Increased efforts to combat overprescribing of doctors in the United States must continue.

Moreover, combating drug addiction requires addressing the root cause of the problem. For decades, the United States has focused on punishing people who are addicted to drugs. The logic was that people who violate the laws should serve time in jail and prison and pay for their crimes. The U.S. government will not solve the addiction crisis by arresting its way out of the problem. Prisons fail to help individuals overcome their addictions, and instead, often serve as the epicenter for drugs (i.e., inmates can obtain drugs if they are willing to pay the right price). Unless individuals can overcome their addiction by participating in the necessary treatment and counseling programs, the United States will continue to face grave public health challenges. More resources are needed to help people in need obtain the necessary mental health services.

Notes

1. The number is based on 2013 estimates; National Institute of Health, "Trends & Statistics," *National Institute of Drug Abuse*, https://www.drugabuse.gov/related-topics/trends-statistics#supplemental-references-for-economic-costs, accessed June 17, 2020; Curtis Florence, Feijun Luo, Likang Xu, and Chao Zhou, "The economic burden of prescription opioid overdose, abuse and dependence in the United States, 2013," *Medical Care* 54, no. 10 (2016): p. 901.

2. For more, see: Brendan. LoPuzzo, "A Bitter Pill to Swallow: The Need for a Clearly-Defined Course of Professional Practice When Prescribing Opioids for the Legitimate Medical Purpose of Treating Pain," *Hofstra Law Review* 47 (2018): pp. 1397–1431; Rebecca Delfino, "Just What the Doctor Ordered: A New Federal Statute to Criminalize Physicians for Overprescribing Opioids," *Loyola Law School*, Los Angeles Legal Studies Research Paper 2020-03 (2020).
3. David Armstrong, "The Family Trying to Escape Blame for the Opioid Crisis," *The Atlantic*, April 10, 2018.
4. Patrick Radden Keefe, "The Family that Built an Empire of Pain," *The New Yorker*, October 23, 2017; David Armstrong, "The Family Trying to Escape Blame for the Opioid Crisis."
5. David Armstrong, "The Family Trying to Escape Blame for the Opioid Crisis."
6. Joanna Walters, "Meet the Sacklers: the family feuding over blame for the opioid crisis," *The Guardian*, February 13, 2018; for more, see: Greg H. Jones, Eduardo Bruera, Salahadin Abdi, and Hagop M. Kantarjian, "The opioid epidemic in the United States—Overview, origins, and potential solutions," *Cancer* 124, no. 22 (2018): pp. 4279–4286; Tim Schwab, "US opioid prescribing: the federal government advisers with recent ties to big pharma," *Bmj* 366 (2019): pp. l5167.
7. Quoted in Patrick Radden Keefe, "The Family that Built an Empire of Pain"; for more, see: Scott H. Podolsky, David Herzberg, and Jeremy A. Greene, "Preying on Prescribers (and Their Patients)—Pharmaceutical Marketing, Iatrogenic Epidemics, and the Sackler Legacy," *New England Journal of Medicine* 380, no. 19 (2019): pp. 1785–1787.
8. Katie Warren and Taylor Nicole Rogers, "The family behind OxyContin pocketed $10.7 billion from Purdue Pharma. Meet the Sacklers, who built their $13 billion fortune off the controversial opioid," *Business Insider*, March 23, 2020; Hillary Hoffower, "The 28 richest American families, ranked," *Business Insider*, July 31, 2019.
9. For more, see: Norman S. Miller, "Failure of enforcement controlled substance laws in health policy for prescribing opiate medications: a painful assessment of morbidity and mortality," *American Journal of Therapeutics* 13, no. 6 (2006): pp. 527–533.
10. Quoted in Chris McGreal, "Why were millions of opioid pills sent to a West Virginia town of 3,000?" *The Guardian*, October 2, 2019.
11. National Institute of Drug Abuse, "West Virginia: Opioid-Involved Deaths and Related Harms," *NIDA*, June 8, 2020, https://www.drugabuse.gov/opioid-summaries-by-state/west-virginia-opioid-involved-deaths-related-harms, accessed June 18, 2020.

12. Chris McGreal, "Why were millions of opioid pills sent to a West Virginia town of 3,000?"
13. Drug Enforcement Administration (DEA), "Pharmaceutical distributor and executives, pharmacists charged with unlawfully distributing painkillers," *DEA*, July 18, 2019.
14. Alene Kennedy-Hendricks, Matthew Richey, Emma E. McGinty, Elizabeth A. Stuart, Colleen L. Barry, and Daniel W. Webster, "Opioid overdose deaths and Florida's crackdown on pill mills," *American Journal of Public Health* 106, no. 2 (2016): pp. 291–297; Robert K. Twillman, "Pill mills are not pain clinics: The challenge of addressing one without harming the other," *Journal of Medical Regulation* 98, no. 2 (2012): pp. 7–11.
15. Department of Justice (DOJ), "Fourteen Individuals Charged for Operating 'Pill Mills' and Illegally Prescribing Drugs to Hundreds of Patients in Multiple Locations in the Philadelphia Area," *DOJ*, February 6, 2019, p. 2.
16. Department of Justice (DOJ), "Fourteen Individuals Charged for Operating 'Pill Mills' and Illegally Prescribing Drugs to Hundreds of Patients in Multiple Locations in the Philadelphia Area," p. 2.
17. Drug Enforcement Administration (DEA), "Pill mill clinic manager sentenced to nine years in federal prison for illegal opioid distribution," *DEA*, June 10, 2019.
18. National Institute on Drug Abuse (NIH), "Overdose Death Rates," *NIH*, https://www.drugabuse.gov/drug-topics/trends-statistics/overdose-death-rates, accessed June 29, 2020.
19. Holly Hedegaard, Arialdi M. Miniño, and Margaret Warner, "Drug Overdose Deaths in the United States, 1999–2018," *Center for Disease Control and Prevention*, NCHS Data Brief No. 356, January 2020.
20. Jessica Bursztynsky, "Americans more likely to die from opioid overdose today than car accident," *CNBC*, January 16, 2019.
21. Center for Disease Control and Prevention (CDC), "2017 Drug Overdose Death Rates," *CDC*, https://www.cdc.gov/drugoverdose/data/statedeaths/drug-overdose-death-2017.html, accessed June 29, 2020.
22. Quoted in Dan Levin, "The Class of 2000 'Could Have Been Anything,'" *The New York Times*, December 2, 2019.
23. Quoted in Dan Levin, "The Class of 2000 'Could Have Been Anything.'"
24. Quoted in Dan Levin, "The Class of 2000 'Could Have Been Anything.'"
25. Jennifer Harlan, "'You Can Make It Out': Readers Share Stories of Opioid Addiction and Survival," *The New York Times*, December 27, 2018.
26. For more, see: Julie Netherland and Helena Hansen, "White opioids: Pharmaceutical race and the war on drugs that wasn't," *BioSocieties* 12, no. 2 (2017): pp. 217–238; Anjali Om, "The opioid crisis in black and white:

the role of race in our nation's recent drug epidemic," *Journal of Public Health* 40, no. 4 (2018): pp. e614–e615.
27. Jennifer Harlan, "'You Can Make It Out': Readers Share Stories of Opioid Addiction and Survival."
28. Patrick McElwaine, "Dear Recovery, You Saves My Life," *NAMI Virtual Forum*, April 23, 2020, https://www.youtube.com/watch?time_continue=1&v=6GSwEF7qlv0&feature=emb_title, accessed June 29, 2020.
29. Nicholas J. Somerville, Julie O'Donnell, R. Matthew Gladden, Jon E. Zibbell, Traci C. Green, Morgan Younkin, Sarah Ruiz et al., "Characteristics of fentanyl overdose—Massachusetts, 2014–2016," *MMWR. Morbidity and mortality weekly report* 66, no. 14 (2017): p. 382.
30. Drug Enforcement Administration (DEA), *Drugs of Abuse: A DEA Resource Guide 2017 Edition* (Washington, DC: DEA, 2017).
31. Center for Disease Control and Prevention, "Synthetic Opioid Overdose," *CDC*, https://www.cdc.gov/drugoverdose/data/fentanyl.html, accessed July 18, 2020. Julie K. O'Donnell, John Halpin, Christine L. Mattson, Bruce A. Goldberger, and R. Matthew Gladden, "Deaths involving fentanyl, fentanyl analogs, and U-47700—10 states, July–December 2016," *MMWR. Morbidity and mortality weekly report* 66, no. 43 (2017): p. 1197; Julie O'Donnell, R. Matthew Gladden, Christine L. Mattson, and Mbabazi Kariisa, "Notes from the field: overdose deaths with carfentanil and other fentanyl analogs detected—10 states, July 2016–June 2017," *Morbidity and Mortality Weekly Report* 67, no. 27 (2018): p. 767; WHYY, "Highly toxic drug carfentanil detected in recent Philadelphia opioid deaths," *WHYY*, July 12, 2017.
32. T. J. Portas, "A review of drugs and techniques used for sedation and anaesthesia in captive rhinoceros species," *Australian Veterinary Journal* 82, no. 9 (2004): pp. 542–549; WHYY, "Highly toxic drug carfentanil detected in recent Philadelphia opioid deaths," *WHYY*, July 12, 2017.
33. Aubrey Whelan, "How Philly plans to combat the nation's worst big-city opioid crisis in 2020," *Philadelphia Inquirer*, January 21, 2020.
34. Quoted in Jennifer Percy, "Trapped by the 'Walmart of Heroin,'" *The New York Times*, October 10, 2018.
35. Quoted in Jennifer Percy, "Trapped by the 'Walmart of Heroin.'"
36. Quoted in Jennifer Percy, "Trapped by the 'Walmart of Heroin.'"
37. Quoted Jennifer Percy, "Trapped by the 'Walmart of Heroin.'"
38. Daniel Craig, "Philly sees big increase in gang activity, feds say," *Philly Voice*, December 7, 2016; National Drug Intelligence Center U.S. Department of Justice (NDIC), *Drug Market Analysis: Philadelphia/Camden High Intensity Drug Trafficking Area* (Washington, DC: NDIC, 2008).

39. Philadelphia Police Department, "Crime Map & Stats," *Philadelphia PD*, https://www.phillypolice.com/crime-maps-stats/, accessed June 29, 2020.
40. Stephanie Farr and Harold Brubaker, "19 shootings, 28 victims, 5 dead as Philly weekend violence escalates," *Philadelphia Inquirer*, June 17, 2019.
41. Quoted in Sandra E. Garcia, "Philadelphia Shootings Kill Girl, 2, and Wound Boy, 11 Months, Police Say," *The New York Times*, October 21, 2019.
42. Quoted in Sandra E. Garcia, "Philadelphia Shootings Kill Girl, 2, and Wound Boy, 11 Months, Police Say."
43. The Federal Bureau of Investigation (FBI): Philadelphia Divisions, "Leader of Violent City Drug Gang Sentenced," *FBI*, April 03, 2012, https://archives.fbi.gov/archives/philadelphia/press-releases/2012/leader-of-violent-city-drug-gang-sentenced, accessed June 29, 2020.
44. George Anastasia, "Kensington man convicted of running longtime narcotics network," *The Philadelphia Inquirer*, November 30, 2011.
45. Quoted in U.S. Attorneys » Eastern District of Pennsylvania, Department of Justice (DOJ), "Leader of Violent Drug Trafficking Gang from North Philadelphia Sentenced to 30 Years in Prison," *DOJ*, November 21, 2019, https://www.justice.gov/usao-edpa/pr/leader-violent-drug-trafficking-gang-north-philadelphia-sentenced-30-years-prison, accessed June 29, 2020.
46. Michaela Winberg, "Philly's Safehouse to open nation's first supervised injection site after judge clearance," *Billy Penn*, February 25, 2020.
47. Quoted in Safehouse, "Frequently Asked Questions," *Safehouse*, https://www.safehousephilly.org/frequently-asked-questions#faqgeneral-services, accessed June 29, 2020.
48. Quoted in Bobby Allyn, "Philadelphia Nonprofit Opening Nation's 1st Supervised Injection Site Next Week," *NPR*, February 26, 2020.
49. United States Code, 2011 Edition, "Title 21 – Food and Drugs. Chapter 13-Drug Abuse Prevention and Control. Subchapter 1-Control and Enforcement. Part D-Offenses and Penalties. Sec. 865"; Michael E. Rayfield, "Pure Consumption Cases under the Federal 'Crackhouse' Statute," *The University of Chicago Law Review* 75, no. 4 (2008): pp. 1805–1832.
50. Abby Goodnough, "Safe Injection Site for Opioid Users Faces Trump Administration Crackdown," *The New York Times*, February 6, 2019.
51. Safehouse, "Frequently Asked Questions."
52. Aubrey Whelan, "How Philly plans to combat the nation's worst big-city opioid crisis in 2020."
53. Bobby Allyn, "Philadelphia Nonprofit Opening Nation's 1st Supervised Injection Site Next Week," *NPR*, February 26, 2020.

54. Abby Goodnough, "Safe Injection Site for Opioid Users Faces Trump Administration Crackdown;" Sharon Larson, Norma Padron, Jennifer Mason, Tyler Bogaczyk, Supervised Consumption Facilities –Review of the Evidence (Philadelphia, PA: Main Line Health System, 2017).
55. Steven Dudley, Deborah Bonello, Jaime López-Aranda, Mario Moreno, Tristian Clavel, Bjorn Kjelstad, Juan José Restrepo, *Mexico's Role in The Deadly Rise of Fentanyl* (Washington, DC: Wilson Center, 2019).
56. Ben Westhoff, "The Brazen Way a Chinese Company Pumped Fentanyl Ingredients Into the U.S.," *The Atlantic*, August 18, 2019; Steven Lee Myers, "China Cracks Down on Fentanyl. But Is It Enough to End the U.S. Epidemic?" *The New York Times*, December 1, 2019; Vanda Felbab-Brown, *Fentanyl and geopolitics: Controlling opioid supply from China* (Washington, DC: Brookings Institution, 2020).
57. Drug Enforcement Administration (DEA), *Fentanyl Flow to the United States* (Springfield, VA: DEA, 2020).
58. Steven Lee Myers, "China Cracks Down on Fentanyl. But Is It Enough to End the U.S. Epidemic?"
59. Steven Lee Myers, "China Sentences Man to Death for Trafficking Fentanyl to the U.S.," *The New York Times*, November 7, 2019.
60. Steven Dudley, Deborah Bonello, Jaime López-Aranda, Mario Moreno, Tristian Clavel, Bjorn Kjelstad, Juan José Restrepo, *Mexico's Role in The Deadly Rise of Fentanyl*.
61. U.S. Customs and Border Protection, "CBP Enforcement Statistics Fiscal Year 2020," U.S. *Customs and Border Protection*, https://www.cbp.gov/newsroom/stats/cbp-enforcement-statistics, accessed June 29, 2020.
62. Matt Belvedere, "Ex-Mexican President Vicente Fox: The idea of a border wall is 'stupidity out of the mind of Trump,'" *CNBC*, April 23, 2018; Jessica Becker, "Speaking to The Wall: Reconceptualizing the US–Mexico Border 'Wall' from the Perspective of a Realist and Constructivist Theoretical Framework in International Relations," *Journal of Borderlands Studies* (2018): pp. 1–13; John Patrick Leary, "Decoding "build the wall": What liberal critics miss," *NACLA Report on the Americas* 49, no. 2 (2017): pp. 146–148; Massimiliano Demata, "'A great and beautiful wall': Donald Trump's populist discourse on immigration," *Journal of Language Aggression and Conflict* 5, no. 2 (2017): pp. 274–294.
63. Quinn Owen, "Border wall construction plows through southwestern US undeterred by COVID-19," *ABC News*, May 13, 2020.
64. John Burnett, "$11 Billion And Counting: Trump's Border Wall Would Be The World's Most Costly," *NRP*, January 19, 2020.
65. Quoted in John Burnett, "$11 Billion And Counting: Trump's Border Wall Would Be The World's Most Costly."

66. Quoted in Quinn Owen, "Border wall construction plows through southwestern US undeterred by COVID-19."
67. Bureau of Transportation Statistics, "Border Crossing/Entry Data," *Bureau of Transportation Statistics*, https://www.bts.gov/content/border-crossingentry-data, accessed June 29, 2020.
68. For more, see: "Border Crossing Entry Data: 2019 Ranking," https://explore.dot.gov/views/BorderCrossingData/CrossingRank?:isGuestRedirectFromVizportal=y&:embed=y, accessed June 29, 2020.
69. "Broder Crossing Entry Data: Monthly Data," https://explore.dot.gov/views/BorderCrossingData/Monthly?:isGuestRedirectFromVizportal=y&:embed=y, accessed June 29, 2020.

CHAPTER 5

Prisons and the Consequences of Tough on Crime Policies at Home and Abroad

Abstract This chapter concentrates on the linkages between the war on drugs and the prison population in the United States and in the Americas. It highlights the impact of three-strike laws and addresses other important topics, such as race, women, drugs, and the increasing prison population. This chapter sheds light on the challenges of recidivism and provides data about the cost of the massive prison population. It also stresses that prosecutorial discretion has been a contributing factor in the increasing prison population, not just the war on drugs. This chapter then turns to trends in prison in other countries in the Americas, highlighting the impact of the drug war on the incarceration populations.

Keywords Prison • Americas • Three-strikes • Tough on crime • Policies • Fear

In 2013, the court sentenced Virginia Mireles, someone who has not been a stranger to the criminal justice system, to five years for property crimes. According to Mireles, "Any crime I've ever committed has been in regard to getting my fix."[1] This chapter examines cases like Virginia Mireles to better understand the trends in incarceration in the Americas and the intricate linkages between the war on drugs and the prison system. The United States, and many other Latin American countries, has attempted to solve the problems of drug consumption and trafficking through incarceration.

© The Author(s), under exclusive license to Springer Nature Switzerland AG 2021
J. D. Rosen, *The U.S. War on Drugs at Home and Abroad*, https://doi.org/10.1007/978-3-030-71734-6_5

The consequence has been a massive increase in the prison populations around the region. Many prisons in the Americas serve as epicenters of criminal activity and fail to rehabilitate prisoners. This chapter begins with an examination of U.S. policies and trends in incarceration. It examines not only the recent policies but also the cost of the criminal justice system. It then turns to various cases in Latin America, as some governments have used the United States as a model and received financial support from Washington to assist with counternarcotic and criminal justice policies.[2] The result of the iron fist policies has been that prison populations have spiked as many people received excessive sentences for drug-related crimes.

Tough on Crime Policies and the U.S. Prison Explosion

In the United States, the increasing crime rates over time and the role of the media in the 1990s created fear among many Americans. The United States saw spikes in crime from 1960 to 1980 as the number of violent crimes increased by more than 200 percent. Crime in the United States continued to rise over the years. In 1991, for instance, the United States recorded more than 750 offenses per 100,000 people, which sparked fear among society.[3] Many Americans felt afraid to leave their homes, and these feelings of insecurity were compounded by news reports of violence in cities like Los Angeles, California. Nightly news reports about crime and violence sweeping across the United States helped stoke the trepidations of many citizens, who desired for politicians to take drastic measures to reduce crime and insecurity.[4]

Mike Reynolds, a wedding photographer who lived in Fresno California, and his family experienced a tragedy that resulted in the death of their daughter in 1992. Reynolds' daughter was visiting her family as she came home from college to attend a wedding. Two men approached her while she tried to get into her car and attempted to rob her. One of them pulled out a gun and shot her. The fear and anger caused by this tragic event led Reynolds to campaign for tougher laws as both men involved in the killing of Reynolds' daughter had long criminal wrap sheets and could be defined as "career criminals."[5]

Reynolds led the push for three-strikes. Yet his quest for change fell on deaf ears until Richard Allen Davis kidnapped Polly Klaas, who was 12 years old at the time, from a quiet neighborhood in Petaluma, California.

The search for Polly lasted for two months and grabbed national attention as the media covered the evolution in the case. The case ended in tragedy. Polly's father told the media that "America's Child is dead." Her killer had a long criminal history, including two convictions for kidnapping, and had recently been released from prison. This led scores of Americans to question how this tragedy occurred, and they blamed the criminal justice system for releasing this violent career criminal who strangled an innocent young girl. Reynolds' petition for three-strikes received 80,000 signatures after these tragic events, and the new law passed in California.[6]

For decades, politicians in the United States worried about being labeled "soft on crime." Politicians ran—and continue to campaign—on the platforms focused on the need to implement the rule of law and incarcerate criminals. Combating crime, however, has not only been a focus for Republicans but rather tough on crime policies have been a bipartisan issue. In fact, President Clinton signed into law the Violent Crime Control and Law Enforcement Act of 1994,[7] often referred to as the 1994 Crime Bill, which sentenced people to 25 years to life in prison after their third felony offense. He told Congress:

> When I sign this crime bill, we together are taking a big step toward bringing the laws of our land back into line with the values of our people and beginning to restore the line between right and wrong. There must be no doubt about whose side we're on. People who commit crimes should be caught, convicted, and punished. This bill puts Government on the side of those who abide by the law, not those who break it; on the side of the victims, not their attackers; on the side of the brave men and women who put their lives on the line for us every day, not the criminals or those who would turn away from law enforcement. That's why police and prosecutors and preachers fought so hard for this bill and why I am so proud to sign it into law today.
>
> When this bill is law, "three strikes and you're out" will be the law of the land; the penalty for killing a law enforcement officer will be death; we will have a significant—[applause]— we will have the means by which we can say punishment will be more certain. We will cut the Federal work force over a period of years by 270,000 positions to its lowest level in 30 years and take all that money to pay for this crime bill. The savings will be used to put 100,000 police officers on the street, a 20 percent increase. It will be used to build prisons to keep 100,000 violent criminals off the street. It will be used to give our young people something to say yes to, places where they can go after school where they are safe, where they can do constructive

things that will help them to build their lives, where teachers replace gang leaders as role models. All of these things should be done and will be done.[8]

This bill helped President Clinton show that he was not "soft on crime" and that the U.S. government was serious about combating drugs, crime, and violence.

The consequence of the 1994 crime bill has been a proliferation in the United States' prison population,[9] which has continued to increase over time. In 1980, the United States had 319,598 people in prison. By 2016, the number of people in prison increased to more than 1.5 million. In 1980, the United States had 182,288 people in jail. By 2016, the number increased to more than 740,000, demonstrating the massive spike in the inmate population.[10] The number of prisoners has declined slightly in recent years, but it remains high. In 2018, the United States had 179,898 people in federal prison and 1,285,260 individuals in state prison.[11] Today, the U.S. jails have more people than any other country in the world and has a higher prison population rate than any country around the globe, including authoritarian countries such as Iran, Russia, and China.[12]

Three-strike laws resulted in increases in the number of people serving life sentences.[13] In 1992, for example, just under 70,000 people had a life sentence. This number proliferated to 127,677 in 2003 and 142,727 in 2008. By 2016, 161,957 people had a life sentence. The State of California, where the three-strike initiatives began, had just under 40,000 people serving a life sentence, while Florida had 13,005 inmates. In addition, New York had more than 9500 people serving a life sentence, Georgia had 8776, and Ohio recorded 6515 people (Fig. 5.1).[14]

The criticism of the three-strike laws is that people have been sentenced to 25 years to life in prison for minor crimes committed on their third strike. In 1995, for example, the court sentenced Jerry Dewayne Williams to 25 years to life in prison for violating his third strike by stealing a piece of pizza. His attorney commented, "Mr. Williams will be facing the same sentence as if he'd raped a woman, molested a child or done a carjacking, because the statute does not draw distinctions."[15] Williams was convicted previously for attempted robbery, robbery, unauthorized use of a vehicle, and drug possession. The state labeled him as a violent criminal, too dangerous to be on the streets because of his criminal record.[16] Yet Daniel E. Lungren, the State Attorney General, agreed with this classification, and stated: "This is precisely the type of person 'three strikes and you're out' was aimed at: career criminals. It's a victory for the people of

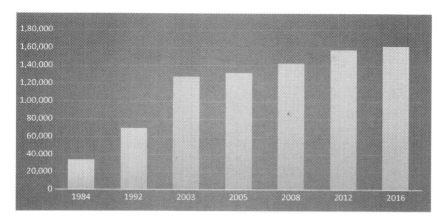

Fig. 5.1 Total number of people serving life sentences. (Source: The Sentencing Project, *Fact Sheet: Trends in U.S. Corrections* (Washington, DC: The Sentencing Project, 2019); A. Nellis, *Still Life: America's Increasing Use of Life and Long-Term Sentences* (Washington, DC: The Sentencing Project, 2016))

California." According to Lungren, this is someone "who has a record of violence in the past – serious felonies – who believes that it's O.K. to go out and terrorize little kids. Most of us are never going to be confronted with a murder or rape in our family. But we at least think our children can sit down in peace in broad daylight, without a 6-foot 4-inch 220-pound ex-con threatening them and taking away food from them."[17] Critics, however, point to this case and contend that this is the law going too far as someone who stole pizza should not spend the rest of his natural life in prison.

In 1995, the court sentenced Jed Harlan Miller to 25 years to life under the three-strike law for stealing a $200 truck and two bicycles. Miller had a history of criminal convictions, although he had never killed anyone. The public defender representing Miller, Charles Gillan, stated: "Jed's main threat to the community is that someone will wake up with their bike missing." He continued, "If that's who 'three strikes' is intended for, then we have a problem in our society."[18] This statement echoes the notion that Miller did not constitute a serious threat to the public, but rather he made a mistake stealing a bike. The three-strike law is intended to lock away the most violent and dangerous criminals that are deemed too dangerous to be on the streets, not someone who committed a petty crime.

Race, Women, Drugs, and Prisons

As scholars such as Michelle Alexander note, the war on drugs and incarceration have created racial disparities in the criminal justice system.[19] One in nine men born in the United States in 2001 will go to prison. The likelihood of a white male born in 2001 being imprisoned is 1 in 17. Yet for African American males born in 2001, the likelihood is much higher: one and three, while it is one and six for Latino men. While women make up less of the prison population, their racial disparities are still present as 1 in 111 Caucasian women born in 2001 end up incarcerated compared to 1 and 18 for African American women and 1 and 45 for Latina women.

The war on drugs also has had a major impact on women, who have a different pathway to prison than men. The number of women in the prison system has increased over several decades. In 1980, the United States had 13,206 women in state and federal facilities. By 2000, this number increased to 93,234. The United States had 112,867 women incarcerated in state and federal prisons in 2010. Most women are in state prisons as they are less likely to commit federal crimes.[20]

The profile of women in prison is different from that of men as most women are involved in non-violent crimes.[21] Research shows that trauma is an underlying factor that is present in many of the cases involving women who are incarcerated. There are different mechanisms that people who have been victims of assault and violence use to cope with pain and trauma, one of which is drug abuse. Instead of sending these individuals to treatment and rehabilitation, the United States has experienced an explosion in the prison population. Most of these prisoners will be released, but the trauma that could have caused them to use drugs is not always addressed in prison and contributes to high recidivism rates.

There are many cases of women who have been sentenced for life in prison for drug-related crimes. While one may assume that people serving life sentences must be three-strike offenders, the fact is that there are people who have been remanded to prison for their natural life after committing their first non-violent drug-related offense. In 1999, for example, Sharanda Jones received a life sentence in federal prison for conspiracy to distribute crack cocaine despite this being her first offense. She was convicted on only one of seven counts even though the prosecutors did not have physical evidence that she had cocaine or sold it. "I remember him saying 'I'm sentencing you to life' and I was just numb," as Jones anticipated that she would have a short prison sentence since the jury did not convict her on the other six counts.[22] Jones was not the only member of her family who received a prison sentence as Ernest, her brother, received an 18-year prison sentence, and her mother received 17 years behind bars.

Jones turned to selling drugs to support her mother and siblings. Her mother suffered from severe health problems after being injured in a car accident, which took away her mobility.[23] She contends:

> Life was very difficult financially. In an attempt to overcome the hardships that accompany poverty, I made a bad decision and began dealing drugs out of desperation to be able to sufficiently support myself and my family. Before incarceration I was ignorant to the harm that drugs inflicted on drug users and their families. I now understand to the fullest level the destruction caused by drugs. I take full responsibility for my actions and know that I deserve to be punished for being involved with dealing drugs and having such a negative impact on the community. But for the rest of my life for my first ever arrest and conviction?[24]

Jones' case reveals that first-time offenders for non-violent drug charges in the United Sates do indeed receive life in prison without the possibility of parole.

Jones' incarceration not only impacted her life but the life of her daughter, Clenesha. Jones started her life sentence when her daughter was eight years old. Clenesha explains the pain and trauma of her mother's incarceration, writing that:

> over 15 years ago, my mother began serving a life sentence with no chance of parole as a first-time non-violent offender. I was 8 years old at the time and my world as I knew it was shattered. Although I didn't understand then that my mother may never be released from prison because she was sentenced to life, I did know that my sunshine was gone. I am now 23-years old and I fully grasp the fact that my mother is set to die in prison for the first crime she ever committed – a non-violent drug crime. I cannot even formulate the right words to express the pain I have felt daily since coming to that harsh realization.[25]

This powerful quote reveals the impact that a life sentence has on one's family as well as the intense levels of frustration given that this constituted a non-violent offense. A life sentence without the possibility of parole is reserved for people that the courts deem too dangerous for society and are not capable of being able to be rehabilitated.

Yet Jones' story has a happy ending. In 2009, Brittany Bird, a law student at the time, vowed to help Jones. In 2015, President Obama commuted Jones' sentence. Jones received a call from Bird who told Jones: "You're going home!" Jones is an advocate for criminal justice reform.[26]

Teresa Griffin is another example of someone who received a life sentence without the possibility for parole for drug charges even though she had no prior criminal record. At the age of 21, Griffin's boyfriend forced her to leave her job and school in Orlando, Florida, and move with him to Texas. Her boyfriend even threatened to kill her after she wanted to end the relationship while pregnant with the couple's child. Griffin's boyfriend later made her transport cocaine between Texas and Oklahoma. When speaking about her life sentence, Griffin contended: "Being sentenced to life without parole was like witnessing my own death. I know I did something wrong, but not enough to take away my life." The life sentence caused her great pain, and she suffered from depression as it is easy to lose hope when there is no possibility of leaving the prison gates alive.[27]

In 2016, the prison warden called Griffin into her office, and Griffin's attorney informed her that President Obama granted her clemency after being incarcerated for almost 25 years. JaneAnne Murray, the leader of a clemency program at the University of Minnesota Law School, worked on this case. In a letter addressed to Griffin, President Obama wrote, "I am granting your application because you have demonstrated the potential to turn your life around."[28] Griffin received a new opportunity on life and has had the ability to reconnect with her family outside the prison gates. She left behind a six-month-old and three other children when the courts sentenced her to life in prison.[29]

Like Griffin, Geneva Cooley received a life sentence without the possibility of parole for a non-violent drug charge. In 2002, Cooley traveled from New York to Alabama and obtained drugs from two individuals. Cooley believes that she was set up as the police stopped her several minutes after the exchange. They searched Cooley and found drugs stashed in her socks. This, however, was not the first time that Cooley had been arrested. She had prior convictions in New York for forgery as she used a stolen credit card and wrote bad checks to support her drug addiction. Cooley received a life sentence without the possibility of parole.

After serving decades in prison, a judge reduced Cooley's sentence. A law school clinic at the University of Alabama worked on Cooley's case for over a year. Her attorneys argued that sentencing someone to life in prison without the possibility of parole for a non-violent drug charge constituted cruel and unusual punishment, which is a violation of the Eighth Amendment.[30] Cooley contended, "They were a good inspiration to me, and they worked diligently to help me get out. And I thank them,"[31] She left prison in Alabama at the age of 72 and is adjusting to life on the outside: "The world is not the same as when I came in here." Cooley continued, "I just want to live the rest of my life in peace with my family."[32]

Another example of drug sentencing disparities involving women is the story of Dorthy Gaines, a former nurse living in Alabama. The police raided her house in 1993 and found drugs, which Gaines did not know existed in her home. Her boyfriend at the time dealt drugs and stored them in her home. The courts sentenced her to more than 19 years in prison. Gains recounts the devastation that this event had on her three children, stating: "My son jumped in the judge's lap at sentencing and asked not to take away his mother."[33] In 2000, Gaines' fate changed as President Clinton commuted her sentence. She has since become an advocate for reform and has not forgotten the countless women who are still incarcerated in Alabama.[34]

The Exorbitant Cost of the Prison System and the Revolving Door

The cost of housing prisoners has continued to increase over time. In 1985, the United States spent $6.7 billion on state corrections. By 1995, this number increased to $26.1 billion. These tough on crime policies have resulted in increasing prison populations and rising costs. State expenditures increased to $51.4 billion and $59.8 billion in 2010 and 2017, respectively.[35] In 2018/2019, it cost a total of $81,203 to house one inmate in the California prison system. Of this more than $81,000, security costs account for $35,425, and inmate healthcare costs totaled $26,665. The other costs include facility operations and records, administration, inmate food and activities, rehabilitation programs, and various miscellaneous fees. It, therefore, is cheaper to send a prisoner to study at Harvard or Yale than it is to incarcerate them in the California prison system.[36]

Critics contend that prisons fail to rehabilitate inmates as six out of every ten people who go to prison will return.[37] Contrary to popular belief, over 90 percent of inmates will leave prison. John Pfaff, a law professor and expert on the criminal justice system, echoes this point, stating: "We're not admitting a few people to an ever-growing pool of long-term inmates; we're basically cycling people in." According to Pfaff, "Every year, about half the prison population leaves, between 600,000 and 700,000 people. But we also admit about the same amount every year. It's a giant churning process."[38]

Moreover, prisons can serve as breeding grounds for predatory behavior and illicit drugs. Inmates can buy and sell drugs on the very lucrative black market operating in prisons throughout the country. One inmate describing the rampant drug flow in prisons contends:

> I guess I was a little naive when I was first locked up, thinking it must be hard to obtain drugs and get high while incarcerated. But to my shock, it was as common or more so than on the outside. (I'm probably in the minority in here because I don't use, it's that pervasive.) Spice, weed, Suboxone, Neurontin, Seroquel, orange peels—people try to get high on whatever they can find, everywhere I've been locked up, and no matter what security measures are in place to prevent it.[39]

This inmate also describes how inmates who are highly addicted to drugs are willing to do anything to feed their addictions:

> And while I went to high school with casual weed smokers and worked at various jobs with weekend coke snorters, I was entirely unprepared for what I've seen in state prison. These are mostly desperate addicts with little else to organize their days around besides the next fix. Getting high is their whole bid. The money they hustle up or that their family sends them, every hard-earned dime of it, is spent on drugs. All they get is small amounts of low-quality stuff, but they'll take it. Because even at the ridiculously high prices this stuff sells for behind bars, that crummy, overpriced little piece will keep the shakes away for another day.[40]

These comments, and insights from many other experts, reveal that prisons often do not function as places where inmates can detox from drugs. Instead, inmates can find drugs as the laws of supply and demand are in full effect behind the prison gates.[41]

Moreover, few prisons in the United States offer access to opioid treatment. Inmates who are trying to avoid drug usage, and are successful, still face the threat of relapsing upon release. Someone who has been using a certain quantity of drugs prior to coming to jail or prison may attempt to take the same dosage upon release, which can cause a fatal overdose. Being released from prison for people suffering from addiction, therefore, can be a dangerous time as intense cravings can lead people to relapse and continue their old habits, but their system is not accustomed to these levels. Researchers have found that the chances of a fatal drug overdose for inmates 14 days after being released are 129 times higher than for a member of the general population, revealing the dangers that inmates returning to society face.[42]

Experts also note that the stress upon being released from prison can lead recently released inmates to use drugs to cope with their environment. Sarah Wakeman of the Massachusetts General Hospital Substance Use Disorder Initiative echoes this point: "They cross over this threshold of leaving this very artificial environment, going back to their usual environment, and with the incredible stress and burden of having just experienced incarceration and trying to pick up relationships and dealing with barriers with housing and employment and insurance. Not surprisingly, cravings come back, and people often relapse very quickly."[43] Critics of the system contend that prisons fail to help treat addiction and address the underlying problems that increase the vulnerability of inmates as they deal with the realities of trying to survive upon being released into the highly competitive globalized world.[44]

Inmates who leave prison are told to find a job, a place to work, and stay out of trouble. However, people with felony charges are denied public housing. Many landlords do not want to rent an apartment to someone who has a felony charge as they perceive this person as potentially "problematic." Attending school also becomes difficult for convicted felons who are denied financial aid from the federal government. People with felony records often are required to disclose their past convictions. Finding a job is not easy as employers have stigmatized people with felony charges. Many job applications have a box that asks whether you are a convicted felon. There have been movements in recent years to ban the box asking whether you have a criminal record. Philadelphia, for example, enacted the Fair Criminal Record Screening Standards Ordinance in 2011 but made amendments that went into effect in March 2016. This law applies to all employers, except some agencies like the police department, courts, and corrections. The employers, however, can check your criminal background after a conditional offer.[45]

Prosecutorial Discretion and Sentencing

Some experts maintain that scholars studying the war on drugs and prison reform have failed to analyze a key issue: prosecutorial reform. In the United States, around 2400 prosecutors are elected. There are only four states that do not elect prosecutors. These elected prosecutors wield tremendous power, but they are partisan as they have party loyalty and focus on being reelected.[46] Prosecutors who move their way up the system can also have a future in politics. According to Jed Shugerman, "The emergence of the prosecutor's office as a steppingstone for higher office" and had "dramatic consequences in American criminal law and mass incarceration."[47]

Prosecutors seeking to move up the ranks or perhaps become a judge are rewarded for conviction rates and locking up defendants, not throwing out cases. Prosecutors will not move up the hierarchy if they are perceived as "soft on crime." Given the high number of cases that prosecutors have, they plea out more than 95 percent of criminal cases.[48] Jail or prison time for the defendant in the case still counts as a win for the prosecutor and helps them improve their record. Emily Bazelon, a staff writer at *The New York Times Magazine* and graduate of Yale Law School, reiterates this point: "What we didn't talk about, or even realize, was that mandatory minimum sentences turn the punishment into the charge. Charging is the job of prosecutors. Judges are not involved in that at all. That gave prosecutors a new role and a new kind of leverage. They use that leverage to induce more and more plea bargains, so you see plea bargaining go way up around this same time."[49] Prosecutors, therefore, can determine whether a charge is dropped or elevated to a higher category. This provides prosecutors with tremendous authority over the lives of millions of Americans.

Some prosecutors have come out publicly and stated that prosecutorial discretion could help save lives.[50] Prosecutors, for example, can choose whether to charge a youth as an adult or a juvenile, which has major implications in terms of the law and potential sentences. Instead of sending first-time offenders for drug possession charges to adult prison and giving them a permanent red flag next to their name as a convicted felon, these individuals could be re-routed into treatment and rehabilitation programs.

Prisons in the Americas, the Drug War, and Tough on Crime Policies Abroad

Tough on crime policies are not only occurring in the United States. Other countries in the Americas—often modeling their prison systems after the United States as well as receiving advice from academics and consultants on the criminal justice system—are experiencing similar trends. Latin America is home to the most violent countries in the world.[51] Populations have demanded tough on crime strategies to combat gangs, crime, and violence. This, however, has had severe repercussions on the prison system. Some prisons in Latin America are operating at several hundred percent of capacity and have served as universities of crime as organized crime leaders dominate prisons and control operations while incarcerated.

Latin America has seen many politicians across the region who have vowed to combat organized crime and increased security.[52] The policies have sent people to prison for decades for drug-related crimes. These policies have led to a proliferation in the prison populations. Many individuals who are in prison for drug trafficking are minor players in organized crime, but they are housed with criminals who have committed a litany of crimes. In addition, there are percentages of inmates who are addicted to drugs and could be re-routed to treatment and rehabilitation. Yet non-discriminatory drug laws have resulted in certain Latin American countries having longer sentences for drug-related crimes than for murder. In Colombia, for instance, someone could serve 60 years for drug-related crimes.[53]

Bolivia is another example of a Latin American country that has faced many challenges with its prison system and the large number of inmates behind bars for drug-related charges. In 1988, the government passed Law 1008, which provided punishments for drug-related crimes. Critics of the law note that it did not distinguish between different types of drug trafficking (e.g., small, medium, and large-scale cases of trafficking).[54] As a result, Bolivia has seen an increase in its prison population from **6065** in 2002 to **9406** in 2010. By 2016, the country had **16,038** prisoners.[55]

WOMEN, DRUG CRIMES, AND PRISONS IN THE AMERICAS

Harsh drug laws have impacted women as more females have become incarcerated for drug-related crimes. Argentina, Brazil, Costa Rica, and Peru have more than 60 percent of female inmates in prison incarcerated for drug-related charges. As of 2016, Mexico has 9601 women detained in more than 1000 state and federal prisons.[56] The majority of women are incarcerated for "health-related crime," which involves drug trafficking. Research on women in the prison system reveal that women are at the lowest levels of the drug trafficking hierarchy. Women have been involved in the transportation of drugs, often for financial necessity. Women often are not major leaders of transnational organized crime groups, but rather they commit these crimes out of financial need as many of them come from marginalized socioeconomic backgrounds.

Many of the women in Latin American prisons come from environments plagued by trauma and domestic violence. There have been cases of forced trafficking and sexual exploitation. Yet tough on crime policies have not taken into consideration the underlying elements that force some women into partaking in illicit economies. Isabel Blas notes, "They talk about imparting justice but a gender perspective is not applied in these cases, and in other cases judges are much tougher on women because they are not fulfilling the role of the good mother, the caregiver, and give them much harsher sentences. There are also women who are rebels or simply drug consumers, but they wind up with years-long prison sentences."[57] Instead of re-routing some of these women for treatment and rehabilitation and alternative forms of punishment, many women in Latin America are serving long-prison sentences. They will return to society with a criminal record and face the same conditions that contributed to them partaking in small-scale trafficking (i.e., poverty, marginalization, and violence).

There are countless examples of women who have been incarcerated for minor-level drug trafficking. As of 2016, most women in Bolivia, 56 percent, were in prison for drug trafficking, while 15 percent were incarcerated for the transportation of drugs.[58] For instance, members of the Andean Information Network (AIN) and the Washington Office on Latin America (WOLA) interviewed a 28-year-old from Cochabamba, Bolivia, who received eight years in prison for transporting three kilograms of cocaine paste. She came from a background plagued by poverty and abuse. Her father also had been convicted of transporting drugs.[59] She notes, "Out of prison my father spent all his wages on alcohol. My mother worked as a seamstress making polleras—traditional skirts—but it was not enough to make ends meet." A friend gave this individual the opportunity to transport drugs to Chile. She contends, "My first time, I carried 900 grams of cocaine. The man coming with us on the trip made me practice by swallowing pieces of carrots 10 centimeters long…I made enough money to buy a bed and some other things, because I didn't have anything."[60]

Furthermore, law enforcement and prosecutors must do a better job of identifying cases of human trafficking, exploitation, forced drug trafficking, and forced labor. As organized crime groups diversify their criminal activities, there will be more cases of human trafficking. Some women who are victims are charged as criminals and incarcerated in prisons throughout the Americas. Police officers as well as prosecutors need to identify these cases and work with victims to prosecute traffickers. This is often quite difficult because victims do not want to talk to the police or prosecutors as traffickers threaten to harm victims and their families. Unless there is more training, education, and resources, police will continue to arrest a percentage of the women[61] who should be treated as victims and provided with treatment and rehabilitation as opposed to serving lengthy sentences for a variety of criminal endeavors such as drug trafficking.

The high levels of overcrowding as well as the dilapidated conditions of many prisons enable many criminal groups to thrive within the penitentiary system. There are prisons in Latin America where inmates oversee many functions of the prison system. This has enabled criminal groups to serve as the de facto authorities in prisons, making it difficult to control what happens behind the prison gates. Steven Dudley and James Bargent maintain, "In other prison systems such as Venezuela, the prison authorities' inability to perform basic functions means criminal networks have stepped in to run operations such as the acquisition and distribution of food and medical supplies, thus increasing their power and influence along with the legitimacy of their role as the true prison authorities."[62] The levels of self-governance and criminal activity that occur in some prisons may lead one to question who is in charge of the prison system, the guards or the inmates.

Some prisons in Latin America have become epicenters of crime. In El Salvador, for instance, tough on crime strategies have led to massive increases in the prison population. Prison officials separated gang members as placing MS-13 gang members with their archrival, the 18th Street gang, would result in violence and potentially even riots. Experts, such as

José Miguel Cruz, note that this policy has had inadvertent ramifications. Gang members from different cliques, or cells, around El Salvador served time in the same prison cells and sectors within the penitentiary system. This has enabled the leaders to organize and strengthen the gang's hierarchy. Gang members are expected to serve time in prison and often view the prison system as a "learning experience" as young gang members can learn from the leadership, many of whom are incarcerated behind bars.[63]

Today, many extortion cases in Mexico occur from behind prison walls. Prisoners spend hours on end calling people on the outside and extorting them for money. The guards, who are often underpaid and outnumbered, allow the prisoners to operate their operations without interruptions. As discussed in the chapter on Mexico, there have been major kingpins, such as Joaquín "El Chapo" Guzmán, who have even escaped.

Prisons in Latin America have even seen lavish parties. In 2013, for example, the San Antonio prison in Venezuela opened a nightclub for inmates to enjoy.[64] The inmates used their smartphones to invite family and friends via social media as the party had a DJ and dancers. The 2011 party followed an infamous festivity behind prison walls that had swimming pools, drugs, alcohol, and a barbecue.[65] The infamous parties show that the prisoners, not the authorities, control what happens behind bars. Fernando Acosta, a Mexican pilot in Venezuela, stated: "The Venezuelan prisoners here run the show, and that makes life inside a bit easier for us all." Another inmate arrested for drug smuggling, Paul Makin, describes the number of weapons behind bars, contending: "I was in the army for 10 years, I've played with guns all my life." According to Makin, "I've seen some guns in here that I've never seen before. AK-47s, AR-15s, M-16s, Magnums, Colts, Uzis, Ingrams. You name them, it's in here."[66] The prisons, like many other detention centers in the region, are not serving as penitentiary systems but rather centers of crime where inmates with serious charges are housed in the same facilities and can better organize their criminal operations.

Understanding the Needs of the Prison Population at Home and Abroad

Many prisons in the Americas fail to rehabilitate their inmate populations because they are overcrowded and plagued by crime and violence. The prison system is in dire need of funding, yet politicians often find it difficult to make an argument for the necessity to fund corrections and find little sympathy for the drastic conditions of prisoners behind bars. Politicians campaigning on tough on crime strategies seek to get re-elected because they are attempting to decrease crime and violence on the street. Prisons, therefore, are often underfunded as it becomes a difficult campaign slogan to sell to voters.

Not only do prisons need to focus on providing inmates with tangible skills, but they must address many of the underlying issues that brought people to prison. There is also a need to understand the inmate populations and how the needs of men and women are different. Criminal Justice scholars have focused on gender-specific programming and the reasons why the needs of incarcerated men and women are distinct. Many of the women charged with drug transportation and minor-scale trafficking are from marginalized communities and are not major players in transnational organized crime. Another major trend has been that these women have suffered different forms of trauma (e.g., domestic violence, emotional abuse, and sexual assault). Gender-specific programming focuses on addressing these underlying needs. WOLA provides a list of some gender-sensitive programming, some of which include the following:

- Reform sentencing requirements to ensure proportionality, distinguishing between low-, mid- and high-level drug offenses; rank in the criminal organization; and non-violent versus violent crimes
- Remove the legislative and practical obstacles preventing those who have committed drug offenses from benefitting from alternatives to incarceration, and guarantee that women who are first-time offenders of low-level, drug-related offenses can enter programs outside the criminal justice system.
- Accompany these measures with the development of a social and community support network that includes education, work, housing, health services, and other programs so as to address the socio-economic factors that lead women to become involved in drug markets in the first place.
- Ensure that these women have access to effective and affordable legal council, and that judicial officials incorporate a gender perspective in order to allow for the possibility of a reduced sentence and alternatives to incarceration. Toward that end, the following factors should be taken into account: poverty and social exclusion, motherhood and caregiver status in relation to other dependent persons, status as

head of household, illiteracy, level of education, lack of job training, immigration status, gender violence, or physical or mental disabilities that may have contributed to the involvement in criminal conduct.
- Implement the necessary training, institutional restructuring, funding streams, and oversight mechanisms to ensure effective implementation of these justice sector reforms.
- Design and carry out strategies for raising community awareness of the need to promote drug policy reforms with a gender perspective.[67]

If these needs are not met, the prisoners who are released will eventually return to prison.

Implementing gender-specific programming requires investing resources in the prison system. Correction officers also need to be trained about such practices. This also requires training other prison staff and hiring the appropriate personnel needed to implement such policies. Research shows that these policies—when implemented correctly—can be effective and address the underlying needs of women.[68]

Conclusion

The United States has seen a large spike in the prison population as a result of the war on drugs and punitive drug policies. The prison system costs the United States billions of dollars per year. There is a need to increase the number of people who can be diverted from the prison system, particularly non-violent drug offenders, who would be better served addressing the underlying problem of drug addiction that led to their criminal convictions. In addition, more people should be paroled to avoid overcrowding and decrease the cost of the prison system.

Prisons in the Latin American cases examined in this chapter require major reforms. The prison system often serves as criminal epicenters. The tough on crime policies in Mexico and El Salvador, for instance, have led to increases in the prison populations. Many of the top leaders of the criminal underworld control their operations while incarcerated. Some of the prisons are operating at several hundred percent of capacity, which has led many critics to argue that the prisons are violating the basic human rights of inmates. Unless major reforms are implemented, it is highly likely that the prison system will continue to face issues of overcrowding and be characterized as criminal recruitment and operations centers.

Notes

1. Quoted in Jeremy Duda, "Sentencing reform debate shines light on lack of substance abuse treatment in prisons," *AZ Mirror*, January 3, 2020.
2. Ethan A. Nadelmann, "US drug policy: A bad export," *Foreign Policy* 70 (1988): pp. 83–108; Maureen Norton-Hawk, "Exporting gender injustice: The impact of the US war on drugs on Ecuadorian women," *Critical Criminology* 18, no. 2 (2010): pp. 133–146; D. Brian Bogges, "Exporting United States Drug Law: An Example of the International Legal Ramifications of the War on Drugs," BYU Law Review (1992): pp. 165–190; Bruce Michael Bagley, "The new hundred years war? US National security and the war on drugs in Latin America," *Journal of Interamerican Studies and World Affairs* 30, no. 1 (1988): pp. 161–182.
3. Lauren-Brooke Eisen, "The 1994 Crime Bill and Beyond: How Federal Funding Shapes the Criminal Justice System," *Brennan Center for Justice*, September 9, 2019, https://www.brennancenter.org/our-work/analysis-opinion/1994-crime-bill-and-beyond-how-federal-funding-shapes-criminal-justice, accessed May 21, 2020; James Austin and Lauren-Brooke Eisen with James Cullen and Jonathan Frank, *How Many Americans Are Unnecessarily Incarcerated?* (New York, NY: Brennen Center for Justice, 2016); Matthew Friedman, Ames C. Grawert, and James Cullen, *Crime Trends: 1990–2016* (New York, NY: Brennan Center for Justice, 2017); Gallup, "Crime," *Gallup*, https://news.gallup.com/poll/1603/crime.aspx, accessed May 21, 2020.
4. Lauren-Brooke Eisen, "The 1994 Crime Bill and Beyond: How Federal Funding Shapes the Criminal Justice System."
5. *The New York Times*, "3 Strikes and You're Out: After 20 Years, Is the Law Working?" *The New York Times*, https://www.youtube.com/watch?v=k_hTTiT0ATA, accessed May 21, 2020; Kevin Fagan, "20 years after Polly Klaas killing, attitudes change," *SF Gate*, October 2, 2013; Lise Forquer, "California's Three Strikes Law--Should a Juvenile Adjudication Be a Ball or a Strike," *San Diego Law Review* 32 (1995): p. 1297; Robert Clinton Peck, "Ewing v. California: Upholding California's Three Strikes Law," *Pepperdine Law Review* 32 (2004): pp. 191–226; Franklin E. Zimring, "Populism, democratic government, and the decline of expert authority: Some reflections on three strikes in California," *Pac. Law Journal* 28 (1996): pp. 243–256.
6. For more, see: *The New York Times*, "Before Being Sentenced to Die, Killer Disrupts a Courtroom," *The New York Times*, Sept. 27, 1996; Franklin E. Zimring, "Populism, democratic government, and the decline of expert authority: Some reflections on three strikes in California"; The

New York Times, "3 Strikes and You're Out: After 20 Years, Is the Law Working?"
7. Lauren-Brooke Eisen, "The 1994 Crime Bill and Beyond: How Federal Funding Shapes the Criminal Justice System;" Michael Vitiello, "Three strikes: Can we return to rationality," *Journal Criminal Law and Criminology* 87 (1996): p. 395; Brandon K. Applegate, Francis T. Cullen, Michael G. Turner, and Jody L. Sundt, "Assessing public support for three-strikes-and-you're-out laws: Global versus specific attitudes," *Crime & Delinquency* 42, no. 4 (1996): pp. 517–534.
8. Bill Clinton, "Remarks on Signing the Violent Crime Control and Law Enforcement Act of 1994," *Administration of William J. Clinton*, September 13, 1994, https://www.govinfo.gov/content/pkg/PPP-1994-book2/pdf/PPP-1994-book2-doc-pg1539.pdf, accessed May 21, 2020, p. 1540.
9. For more, see: Tomislav V. Kovandzic, John J. Sloan III, and Lynne M. Vieraitis. "'Striking out' as crime reduction policy: The impact of 'three strikes' laws on crime rates in US cities," *Justice Quarterly* 21, no. 2 (2004): pp. 207–239; C. S. Clark, "Prison overcrowding: Will building more prisons cut the crime rate," *Congressional Quarterly Researcher* (1994): pp. 97–120; Alfred Blumstein, "Bringing down the US prison population," *The Prison Journal* 91, no. 3_suppl (2011): pp. 12S-26S; Lauren C. Porter, Shawn D. Bushway, Hui-Shien Tsao, and Herbert L. Smith, "How the US prison boom has changed the age distribution of the prison population," *Criminology* 54, no. 1 (2016): pp. 30–55.
10. The Sentencing Project, *Fact Sheet: Trends in U.S. Corrections* (Washington, DC: Sentencing Project, 2019); Danielle Kaeble and Mary Cowhig, *Correctional Populations in the United States, 2016* (Washington, DC: Bureau of Justice Statistics. Key Statistics: Total Correctional Population, 2018).
11. E. Ann Carson, *Prisoners in 2018* (Washington, DC: U.S. Department of Justice, 2020).
12. Michelle Alexander, *The New Jim Crow: Mass Incarceration in the Age of Colorblindness* (New York, NY: The New Press, 2010).
13. For more, see: Erwin Chemerinsky, "Life in prison for shoplifting: Cruel and unusual punishment," *Human Rights* 31 (2004): p. 11; Victor Hassine, Thomas J. Bernard, Richard McCleary, and Richard Alan Wright, *Life without parole: Living in prison today* (Los Angeles, CA: Roxbury Publishing Company, 1996); Marc Mauer, Ryan S. King, and Malcolm C. Young, *The meaning of "life": Long prison sentences in context* (Washington, DC: Sentencing Project, 2004).
14. The Sentencing Project, *Fact Sheet: Trends in U.S. Corrections* (Washington, DC: The Sentencing Project, 2019); A. Nellis, *Still Life: America's*

Increasing Use of Life and Long-Term Sentences (Washington, DC: The Sentencing Project, 2016).
15. Quoted in The Associated Press, "25 Years for a Slice of Pizza," *The New York Times*, March 5, 1995.
16. The Associated Press, "25 Years for a Slice of Pizza."
17. Quoted in The Associated Press, "25 Years for a Slice of Pizza," p. 2.
18. Quoted Jamie Beckett, "Bike Thief's '3 Strikes' Sentence / Judge says hands tied -- 25 years to life," *SF Gate*, May 4, 1995.
19. See: Michelle Alexander, *The New Jim Crow: Mass Incarceration in the Age of Colorblindness*; Doris Marie Provine, *Unequal under Law: Race in the War on Drugs* (Chicago, IL: University of Chicago Press, 2008); W. Wesley Johnson and Mark Jones, "Probation, race, and the war on drugs: An empirical analysis of drug and non-drug felony probation outcomes," *Journal of Drug Issues* 28, no. 4 (1998): pp. 985–1003; Jeff Yates and Andrew B. Whitford, "Race in the war on drugs: The social consequences of presidential rhetoric," *Journal of Empirical Legal Studies* 6, no. 4 (2009): pp. 874–898.
20. The Sentencing Project, *Fact Sheet: Trends in U.S. Corrections*; S. Minor-Harper, *State and Federal Prisoners, 1925–1985* (Washington, DC: Bureau of Justice Statistics, 1986).
21. For more, see: Jeffrey Fagan, "Women and drugs revisited: Female participation in the cocaine economy," *Journal of Drug Issues* 24, no. 2 (1994): pp. 179–225; Marc Mauer, Cathy Potler, and Richard Wolf, *Gender and Justice: Women, Drugs, and Sentencing Policy* (Washington, DC: Sentencing Project, 1999); Marylee Reynolds, "The war on drugs, prison building, and globalization: Catalysts for the global incarceration of women," *NWSA Journal* 20, no. 2 (2008): pp. 72–95; Vernetta D. Young and Rebecca Reviere, *Women Behind Bars: Gender and Race in US prisons* (Boulder, CO: Lynne Rienner Publishers, 2006).
22. Quoted in Wesley Bruer, "From a life sentence to clemency from Obama," *CNN*, September 2, 2016.
23. Wesley Bruer, "From a life sentence to clemency from Obama."
24. Direct quote from see Saranda Jones'website: http://www.iamsharandajones.org/
25. Direct quote from Saranda Jones'website: http://www.iamsharandajones.org/
26. Quote from Wesley Bruer, "From a life sentence to clemency from Obama."
27. American Civil Liberties Union (ACLU), *A Living Death: Life without Parole for Nonviolent Offenses* (New York, NY: ACLU, 2013); American Civil Liberties Union (ACLU), *More Than 3,200 Serving Life Without Parole for Nonviolent Offenses, Finds ACLU*," ACLU, November 13, 2013, https://www.aclufl.org/en/press-releases/more-3200-serving-

life-without-parole-nonviolent-offenses-finds-aclu, accessed June 29, 2020.
28. Quoted in Stephen Montemayor, "Drug inmate wins release, thanks to University of Minnesota program," *Star Tribune*, July 5, 2016.
29. Stephen Montemayor, "Drug inmate wins release, thanks to University of Minnesota program."
30. Rick Rojas, "Leaving Prison at 72," *The New York Times*, October 28, 2019.
31. Quoted in "UA Law Professors, Students Help Geneva Cooley Receive Parole," *Alabama Law: The University of Alabama*, https://www.law.ua.edu/blog/news/ua-law-professors-students-help-woman-receive-parole/, accessed June 17, 2020.
32. Quoted in Rick Rojas, "Leaving Prison at 72."
33. Quoted in The Sentencing Project, "Dorothy Gaines," *The Sentencing Project*, https://www.sentencingproject.org/stories/dorothy-gaines/, accessed June 17, 2020.
34. Drug Police Alliance, "A Victim Becomes an Activist," *Drug Policy Alliance*, https://www.drugpolicy.org/community/movement/victim-becomes-activist, accessed June 17, 2020.
35. The Sentencing Project, F*act Sheet: Trends in U.S. Corrections*; State Expenditure Report Series (Washington, DC: National Association of State Budget Officers, 2017).
36. Legislative Analyst's Office (LAO), "How much does it cost to incarcerate an inmate?" *LAO*, https://lao.ca.gov/PolicyAreas/CJ/6_cj_inmatecost, accessed June 17, 2020.
37. For more on recidivism, see: Jeremy Travis, *But they all come back: Facing the Challenges of Prisoner Reentry* (Washington, DC: The Urban Institute, 2005); David P. Farrington, and Christopher P. Nuttall, "Prison size, overcrowding, prison violence, and recidivism," *Journal of Criminal Justice* 8, no. 4 (1980): pp. 221–231; Mark S. Fleisher, Scott H. Decker, and G. D. Curry, "Going home, staying home: Integrating prison gang members into the community," *Corrections Management Quarterly* 5 (2001): pp. 65–77; United States Sentencing Commission (USSC), *Recidivism Among Federal Violent Offenders* (Washington, DC: USSC, 2019).
38. Quoted in Juleyka Lantigua-Williams, "Are Prosecutors the Key to Justice Reform?" *The Atlantic*, May 18, 2016.
39. Quoted in Dan Rosen, "The Never-Ending Drug Hustle Behind Bars," *The Marshall Project*, November 07, 2019, https://www.themarshallproject.org/2019/11/07/the-never-ending-drug-hustle-behind-bars, accessed June 17, 2020, p. 2.
40. Quoted in Dan Rosen, "The Never-Ending Drug Hustle Behind Bars," p. 2.

41. For more, see: Stephen E. Lankenau, "Smoke'em if you got'em: Cigarette black markets in US prisons and jails," *The Prison Journal* 81, no. 2 (2001): pp. 142–161. David Skarbek, "Governance and prison gangs," *American Political Science Review* 105, no. 4 (2011): pp. 702–716.
42. German Lopez, "How America's prisons are fueling the opioid epidemic," *VOX*, March 26, 2018; Ingrid A. Binswanger, Marc F. Stern, Richard A. Deyo, Patrick J. Heagerty, Allen Cheadle, Joann G. Elmore, and Thomas D. Koepsell, "Release from prison—a high risk of death for former inmates," *New England Journal of Medicine* 356, no. 2 (2007): pp. 157–165.
43. Quoted in German Lopez, "How America's prisons are fueling the opioid epidemic."
44. For more, see: Will Small, S. Kain, Nancy Laliberte, Martin T. Schechter, Michael V. O'shaughnessy, and Patricia M. Spittal, "Incarceration, addiction and harm reduction: inmates experience injecting drugs in prison," *Substance Use & Misuse* 40, no. 6 (2005): pp. 831–843; Michelle McKenzie, Amy Nunn, Nickolas D. Zaller, Alexander R. Bazazi, and Josiah D. Rich, "Overcoming obstacles to implementing methadone maintenance therapy for prisoners: implications for policy and practice," *Journal of Opioid Management* 5, no. 4 (2009): p. 219; Wayne Gillespie, "A multilevel model of drug abuse inside prison," *The Prison Journal* 85, no. 2 (2005): pp. 223–246.
45. Philadelphia Commission of Human Relations, "Ban the Box FAQ," *Philadelphia Commission of Human Relations*, https://www.phila.gov/HumanRelations/DiscriminationAndEnforcement/Pages/BanTheBoxFAQ.aspx, accessed June 17, 2020.
46. Juleyka Lantigua-Williams, "Are Prosecutors the Key to Justice Reform?"
47. Quoted in David Lat, "How Tough-on-Crime Prosecutors Contribute to Mass Incarceration," *The New York Times*, April 8, 2019.
48. Ellen S. Thomas, "Plea bargaining: The clash between theory and practice," *Loyola Law Review* 20 (1973): pp. 303–312; William J. Stuntz, "Plea bargaining and criminal law's disappearing shadow," *Harvard Law Review* (2004): pp. 2548–2569; Kenneth Kipnis, "Criminal justice and the negotiated plea," *Ethics* 86, no. 2 (1976): pp. 93–106.
49. Quoted in Sean Illing, "How bad prosecutors fuel America's mass incarceration problem," *VOX*, May 15, 2019; Emily Bazelon, *Charged: The New Movement to Transform American Prosecution and End Mass Incarceration* (New York, NY: Random House, 2019).
50. For more, see: David Bjerk, "Making the crime fit the penalty: The role of prosecutorial discretion under mandatory minimum sentencing," *The Journal of Law and Economics* 48, no. 2 (2005): pp. 591–625.

51. For more, see: Hanna S. Kassab and Jonathan D. Rosen, eds., *Violence in the Americas* (Lanham, MD: Lexington Books, 2018).
52. For more on the drug war, see: Bruce Michael Bagley, "The new hundred years war? US national security and the war on drugs in Latin America," *Journal of Interamerican Studies and World Affairs* 30, no. 1 (1988): pp. 161–182.
53. This is according to 2012 data; Rodrigo Uprimny Yepes, Diana Esther Guzmán, and Jorge Parra Norato, *Addicted to Punishment: The disproportionality of drug laws in Latin America* (Bogotá, CO: Centro de Estudios de Derecho, Justicia y Sociedad, Dejusticia, 2013), p. 12.
54. Kathryn Ledebur and Coletta A. *Youngers, Promoting Gender-Sensitive Drug Policies in Bolivia* (Washington, DC: WOLA, 2018).
55. Institute for Criminal Policy Research (ICPR), "World Prison Brief: Bolivia," *ICPR,* http://www.prisonstudies.org/country/bolivia, accessed July 10, 2019.
56. Cecilia Ballesteros, "Mexico's women prisoners: doubly punished for not living up to female roles," *El País,* February 12, 2018; original data from Instituto Nacional de Estadística y Geografía (INEGI).
57. Quoted in Cecilia Ballesteros, "Mexico's women prisoners: doubly punished for not living up to female roles."
58. Kathryn Ledebur and Coletta A. *Youngers, Promoting Gender-Sensitive Drug Policies in Bolivia*; Jorge López, "Synthesis of the Current Situation of People Imprisoned under Law 1008." *Penitentiary Regime of the Bolivian Government,* July 2016.
59. Washington Office on Latin America (WOLA), "Punished for Being Poor," *WOLA,* https://womenanddrugs.wola.org/photo_essay/poverty-and-incarceration/, accessed July 1, 2019.
60. Quoted from Washington Office on Latin America (WOLA), "Punished for Being Poor."
61. It is impossible to know the exact percentage.
62. Steven Dudley and James Bargent, "The Prison Dilemma: Latin America's Incubators of Organized Crime," *InSight Crime,* January 19, 2017, https://www.insightcrime.org/investigations/prison-dilemma-latin-america-incubators-organized-crime/, accessed July 10, 2019, p. 9; Simon Romero, "Where Prisoners Can do Anything Except Leave," *The New York Times,* June 3, 2011.
63. Jonathan D. Rosen and José Miguel Cruz, "Rethinking the Mechanisms of Gang Desistance in a Developing Country," *Deviant Behavior* (2018): pp. 1–15; Jonathan D. Rosen and José Miguel Cruz, "Overcoming Stigma and Discrimination: Challenges for Reinsertion of Gang Members in Developing Countries," *International Journal of Offender Therapy and Comparative Criminology* Vol. 62 No. 15 (2018): pp. 4758–4775.

64. Kyra Gurney, "Latin America's Top 5 Prison Parties," *InSight Crime*, October 27, 2014, https://www.insightcrime.org/news/analysis/latin-america-top-five-prison-parties/, accessed June 17, 2020.
65. Kyra Gurney, "Latin America's Top 5 Prison Parties."
66. Quoted in Simon Romero, "Where Prisoners Can Do Anything, Except Leave," *The New York Times*, June 3, 2011.
67. Quoted from Kathryn Ledebur and Coletta A. *Youngers, Promoting Gender-Sensitive Drug Policies in Bolivia*.
68. Katherine P. Moloney, Brenda J. van den Bergh, and Lars F. Moller, "Women in prison: The central issues of gender characteristics and trauma history," *Public Health* 123, no. 6 (2009): pp. 426–430; Emily M. Wright, Patricia Van Voorhis, Emily J. Salisbury, and Ashley Bauman, "Gender-responsive lessons learned and policy implications for women in prison: A review," *Criminal Justice and Behavior* 39, no. 12 (2012): pp. 1612–1632; Barbara Bloom, Barbara Owen, Elizabeth Piper Deschenes, and Jill Rosenbaum, "Moving toward justice for female juvenile offenders in the new millennium: Modeling gender-specific policies and programs," *Journal of Contemporary Criminal Justice* 18, no. 1 (2002): pp. 37–56.

CHAPTER 6

Conclusion

Abstract This chapter is the concluding chapter. It examines the militarization of the war on drugs and the need to rethink drug-related policies. It focuses on learning the importance of context as opposed to policies that can be exported to other countries. This chapter also highlights the need to reduce corruption and reforms of various institutions. Finally, it highlights some alternative policies that countries have implemented, such as decriminalization.

Keywords Drug treatment • Regulation • Decriminalization • Reforms • Lesson learned • Military

The U.S.-led war on drugs has focused on combating the supply of drugs for decades. Drug trafficking organizations are opportunists and are willing to traffic drugs if there is demand. The U.S. government has spent billions of dollars per year interdicting drugs and spraying coca in other countries. Yet concentrating on combating the supply of drugs misses a large component of the equation. The United States is the number one drug-consuming country in the world and must do more to reduce demand.[1] Reducing demand by treating addiction should be based on science.[2] There are leading academics, physicians, and policy experts who have spent decades studying drug treatment and rehabilitation.[3] Simply declaring the opioid epidemic a national emergency will not solve the

© The Author(s), under exclusive license to Springer Nature Switzerland AG 2021
J. D. Rosen, *The U.S. War on Drugs at Home and Abroad*,
https://doi.org/10.1007/978-3-030-71734-6_6

problem unless federal and state funding is available to support treatment, rehabilitation, and prevention. Politicians should focus on what the subject-matter experts are saying and have them at the head of the table when proposing legislation.

For decades, the United States implemented Drug Abuse Resistance Education, known as DARE. Countless academic studies focused on how the program did not work.[4] This caused tremendous frustration among some academics and policymakers who wondered why people in Washington did not make decisions based on science and policy studies. Indeed, politicians do not live in a vacuum. Ideology and different beliefs impact thinking about drug education. Yet there needs to be an effort to justify funding and make sure that the resources being spent on certain programs are being invested wisely.

Scholars note that the United States is not the only drug-consuming country on the planet, but rather there has been a globalization of drug consumption around the world. Thus, even if the United States decreased the demand for drugs to zero—it is extremely unlikely that this will occur—there is still a high demand for cocaine in other countries in the Americas, such as Argentina and Brazil.[5] The European drug market also represents a lucrative proposition for drug traffickers who can shift where they ship drugs to.

Moreover, this book has addressed the issue of the "the balloon effect." Drug trafficking organizations will continue to adapt their routes and balloon out to other areas of the globe where there is demand. The U.S. government cannot declare "victory" in the war on drugs because drug seizures spiked in one year in one country.[6] Combating drug trafficking and organized crime requires a global approach.

The drug war also requires government officials to learn from policies that have not been effective. As documented in the chapter on Colombia, aerial spraying is not an effective policy. Farmers can plant coca in other areas that are harder to locate from the sky. Even worse, the World Health Organization indicates that the key ingredient used in aerial spraying initiatives causes cancer. Scientists have also pointed to the many environmental consequences of such programs. Yet today the Colombian government is under pressure to reduce cocaine production and trafficking. President Donald Trump stated publicly that Colombia must spray again. A return to this strategy, however, demonstrates that policymakers have not learned the lessons of the past. Instead, some governments take one step forward and two steps backward and continue archaic policies that damage the health and wellbeing of people as well as the environment.

The U.S. drug war has been implemented for 50 years at home and abroad. It is important that policymakers analyze where the money is being invested and what have been the results of different programs. The military has continued to receive high levels of funding in the war on drugs.[7] The military has been used in internal policing operations as a result of the high levels of corruption and distrust in the police forces in many countries in the Americas. Research shows that the police are highly distrusted, while the military in Latin America is one of the most trusted institutions.[8] The deployment of the armed forces to combat drug trafficking and organized crime has contributed to more violence. Drug trafficking organizations have fought with the military in some Latin American countries. This is one important factor contributing to the rising levels of violence in countries like Mexico.

Critics of militarization contend that the military should not be used for internal policing operations. This requires serious reforms to the police in the Americas. One of the first major reforms to the police is the need to pay officers more money.[9] Higher pay will help recruit and retain better officers. Police officers need better training. While countries like Mexico have attempted to reform the police on many occasions, this reform requires not only political will but also resources. These reforms also require excellent leadership at the top of organizations and the purging of corrupt officers.

Context Matters: Lessons Learned

There has been a trend in the United States to export models to other countries around the globe. For instance, the United States touted the successes of Plan Colombia and implemented a "Plan Mexico" to combat drug trafficking and organized crime. While there are many differences between Plan Colombia and what became the Mérida Initiative,[10] these plans have similarities as they focused on combating drug trafficking and organized crime. Both policy initiatives utilized the military to combat internal security problems. The Mexican government did not learn from past failures in other countries and the fact that militarizing the war on drugs will not solve organized crime and violence. Despite advocates touting Plan Colombia as a success, Colombia today produces more than 90 percent of the cocaine arriving to the United States. Colombia also has a plethora of criminal groups that have morphed and diversified their illicit activities.[11]

In addition to government policies and models, individual consultants have made millions talking about strategies to combat organized crime and violence. For example, Rudy Giuliani, the former mayor of New York and presidential candidate, has consulted with governments around the world about how New York City improved its security situation.[12] Giuliani and his associates at his consulting firm have charged millions of dollars to discuss policing strategies to Central American governments. While there are always lessons to be learned about case studies and what other countries have done to combat organized crime, it is important to remember that context matters. San Salvador, El Salvador, is not New York City just like Los Angeles, California, is not San Pedro Sula, Honduras. These cities and countries have different problems and require comprehensive solutions. The resources, agency structures, and methods to combat security problems also are different. In summary, context is important, and "one-size fits all" models that are designed to combat drug trafficking and organized crime will not work everywhere.[13]

Academics and outside consultants working in the Americas and other parts of the world trying to implement reforms to various institutions, such as the police or the prison system, must be aware of the local realities. It is important to partner with local organizations and have a diverse team that understands not only the language but also the history and structural causes that contribute to the issues being examined. Simply importing a model used in another country is often not effective.

Systematic Reforms: Combating Corruption and Impunity

Tackling drug trafficking and violence requires reforming various institutions in the countries examined in this volume. The cases of Colombia and Mexico reveal that organized crime and drug trafficking groups can penetrate the state apparatus and bribe corrupt police officers, judges, and government officials. The case of the 43 missing students in Mexico shows the intricate web of corrupt officials involved in the disappearance of these students from Southern Mexico. Combating corruption requires arresting and prosecuting corrupt officials working in different branches of government. Experts, like Roberto Zepeda and Jorge Chabat, note that reforms must occur across different levels of government.[14] It is not efficient to reform the police if a drug trafficker can then bribe a judge. Thus, it is important that institutions are reformed across the different branches of government.

Reforms, however, do not happen overnight. Meaningful structural reforms can take decades to implement. Government officials must always balance these reforms and think about three time periods: the short-run, medium-run, and long-run. Politicians face pressure to provide immediate solutions to problems. Some policy solutions, such as tough on crime approaches and mandatory minimum sentences, have had drastic impacts on the prison population. It is important for government officials to weigh the potential consequences of each decision and not focus only on scoring points during the next election cycle.

Prison Reform

There is a major need for prison reform in the United States and abroad. This book has shown that prisons in the United States are filled to the brim with low-level offenders. Many people are incarcerated on drug-related charges, non-violent crimes, and probation or parole violations. This book argues that prisons often fail to rehabilitate offenders. In the United States, prison reform has become a bipartisan issue. Republicans and Democrats have been critical of the cost of prisons but also the large number of people behind bars and removed from their community.[15] Not only is the prison system costing billions of dollars per year in the United States, but the majority of prisoners return to prison upon release.

Some countries in Latin America have used the U.S. war on drugs as a model and followed trends in incarceration. Latin American countries have seen drastic spikes in their prison populations. Many prisons serve as schools of crime. In the case of El Salvador, for example, the top members of MS-13 and the 18th Street are behind bars.[16] Gangs have used the prison system to better organize and carry out their activities on the streets. This book has shown that some prisons in Latin America are even controlled by inmates as the guards are not only underpaid and over-worked, but powerful criminal organizations can threaten them.

A Global Approach

Combating drug trafficking and organized crime requires that countries work together. The history of the war on drugs has been filled with finger-pointing and government officials blaming other countries.[17] Scholars like Roberto Zepeda note that there must be cooperation between consuming, transit, and producing countries.[18] The complex nature of drug trafficking and illicit markets will not be addressed unless countries can work together. This, however, is an arduous task as it requires political will and intelligence sharing.

The Donald Trump administration's focus on building a wall between the United States and Mexico will not solve drug trafficking and organized crime. As this book has noted, the wall will not end the flow of drugs. The United States and Mexico are part of the globalized world of the twenty-first century, where cars and trucks pass through checkpoints along the U.S.-Mexico border every day. Indeed, a wall already exists along parts of the U.S.-Mexico border and it does not stop legal entries that exist because of globalization and increasing interconnectedness that began with the signing of the North American Free Trade Agreement. Finally, traffickers have developed other mechanisms to penetrate the U.S.-Mexican border, including tunnels. The notorious leader of the Sinaloa Cartel, Joaquín Guzmán, was famous for having his Sinaloa cartel build tunnels into the United States.[19]

Alternative Drug Control Policies

Different countries around the world have attempted a variety of policies to address drug regulation. In 2001, for example, Portugal decriminalized drugs to address its drug problem and reduce levels of HIV/AIDS infections.[20] It is important to note that decriminalization is different from legalization, as drugs remain illegal. However, people who are caught with drugs will not serve time in prison. Advocates of decriminalization highlight that this approach focuses more on health, treatment, and rehabilitation as opposed to criminalizing addiction.

In the United States, marijuana legalization started at the ballot box. In 2012, Washington and Colorado legalized marijuana for recreational usages.[21] More states continued to legalize marijuana over time. As of November 2020, 15 states and Washington D.C. legalized marijuana for recreational usage, while medical marijuana is legal in more than half of the states in the country. Marijuana, however, remains illegal at the federal level and creates a legal dilemma for the U.S. government. In the United States, federal law trumps state law. Thus, federal agencies like the Drug Enforcement Administration can arrest people for utilizing marijuana in states where it is legal, as marijuana consumers are still violating federal law. This could eventually lead to a Supreme Court case to decide the fate of marijuana.

In November 2020, Oregon became the first state to decriminalize marijuana. In December 2020, the United States House of Representatives passed a bill, known as the Marijuana Opportunity Reinvestment and Expungement Act, or MORE Act, to decriminalize marijuana. Yet the Republican-controlled Senate is not expected to pass the legislation. Jerry Nadler, the House Judiciary Committee Chairman and the sponsor of the bill stated, "Federal action on this issue would follow the growing recognition in the states that the status quo is unacceptable. Despite the federal government's continuing criminalization of marijuana, 36 states and the District of Columbia have legalized medical cannabis. Fifteen states and the District of Columbia have legalized cannabis for adult recreational use."[22] Other Democrats have also supported the bill and maintained that this action is needed, highlighting the racial disparities in the drug war.[23]

Moreover, other countries in the Americas have taken different measures to legalize drugs. Scholars like José Miguel Cruz note that the legalization of marijuana in Uruguay was a top-down initiative, which is the opposite of the policy process in the United States. President José Mujica advocated for the legalization of marijuana and Law 19,172 to address the "production, commercialization, and consumption," of marijuana.[24] The Uruguay case is unique because the populace did not have a consensus regarding this issue, and activists did not play a fundamental role in the passage of this legislation.[25]

Other transit countries have also taken recent initiatives to alter drug laws. In 2018, the Mexican Supreme Court ruled that the state should allow recreational marijuana. The court stated, "But the effects caused by marijuana do not justify an absolute prohibition on its consumption."[26] In November 2020, the Mexican Senate voted in favor of a bill to legalize marijuana. President Andrés Manuel López Obrador's political party supports this initiative.[27] Advocates in favor of this bill maintain that it could reduce the profits of criminal networks and decrease Mexico's prison population.

These aforementioned cases show that different countries have utilized a variety of measures to address drug prohibition. There have been more politicians around the Americas who have maintained that the war on drugs has been a failure.[28] Some of these policies focus on decreasing the prison population and implementing harm reduction approaches as opposed to punitive policies. These case studies can serve as natural experiments, and scholars and policy analysts can study the impact of such policies over time.

Conclusion

There are countless academics and scholars who have written on drug trafficking, organized crime, and addiction.[29] This book has attempted to provide a short introduction to some of the major issues regarding the U.S. war on drugs and the criminal justice system both at home and abroad. The take-away point is that the drug war has not been effective. Politicians and policymakers must learn from the lessons of the past. People often forget history, but it is important to remember to be students of the past and analyze why certain programs have not been effective.

Furthermore, policymaking should be based on evidence-based approaches.[30] Scientists and social scientists using data analysis and evaluating programs and policies have been ignored by some policymakers. Data-driven approaches to studying the effectiveness of different policies—whether it is the war on drugs, Plan Colombia, the Mérida Initiative, the prison system, or drug treatment programs—should continue to be at the forefront. The rejection of science, data, and evidence-based practices by some people in the United States, including the policymaking community, is troubling and should be reformed.

Finally, citizens play an important role in policymaking. Individuals can force change by exercising their right to vote. Politicians can be held accountable for the decisions that they make regarding criminal justice reforms or other policy issues. People can vote out politicians and pressure current ones to hear the opinions of the public. While change can be slow, civic society from journalists to student organizations play an important role in any society.

NOTES

1. For more, see: Gregory Wilson, "The Changing Game: The United States Evolving Supply-Side Approach to Narcotics Trafficking," *Vand. J. Transnat'l L.* 26 (1993): p. 1163; Damon Barrett, "Harm reduction is not enough for supply side policy: A human rights-based approach offers more," *International Journal of Drug Policy* 23, no. 1 (2012): pp. 18–19; David Whynes, "Illicit Drug Production and Supply-side Drugs Policy in Asia and South America," *Development and Change* 22, no. 3 (1991): pp. 475–496; Francisco I. Bastos, Waleska Caiaffa, Diana Rossi, Marcelo Vila, and Monica Malta, "The children of mama coca: Coca, cocaine and the fate of harm reduction in South America," *International Journal of Drug Policy* 18, no. 2 (2007): pp. 99–106; Jonathan Caulkins, and Peter Reuter, "Towards a harm-reduction approach to enforcement," *Safer Communities* 8, no. 1 (2009): p. 9.
2. For more, see: Avram Goldstein and Harold Kalant, "Drug policy: striking the right balance," *Science* 249, no. 4976 (1990): pp. 1513–1521; Daniel Werb, Adeeba Kamarulzaman, M. C. Meacham, Claudio Rafful, Benedikt Fischer, S. A. Strathdee, and Evan Wood, "The effectiveness of compulsory drug treatment: a systematic review," *International Journal of Drug Policy* 28 (2016): pp. 1–9.
3. David N. Nurco, "Drug addiction and crime: a complicated issue," *British Journal of Addiction* 82, no. 1 (1987): p. 7; Charles C. Thornton, Edward Gottheil, Stephen P. Weinstein, and Rivka S. Kerachsky, "Patient-treatment matching in substance abuse: Drug addiction severity," *Journal of Substance Abuse Treatment* 15, no. 6 (1998): pp. 505–511; Christy K. Scott, Michael L. Dennis, Alexandre Laudet, Rodney R. Funk, and Ronald S. Simeone, "Surviving drug addiction: the effect of treatment and abstinence on mortality," *American Journal of Public Health* 101, no. 4 (2011): pp. 737–744.
4. For more, see: Susan T., Ennett, Nancy S. Tobler, Christopher L. Ringwalt, and Robert L. Flewelling, "How effective is drug abuse resistance education? A meta-analysis of Project DARE outcome evaluations," *American Journal of Public Health* 84, no. 9 (1994): pp. 1394–1401; Richard R. Clayton, Anne M. Cattarello, and Bryan M. Johnstone, "The effectiveness of Drug Abuse Resistance Education (Project DARE): 5-year follow-up results," *Preventive Medicine* 25, no. 3 (1996): pp. 307–318; Dennis P. Rosenbaum, and Gordon S. Hanson. "Assessing the effects of school-based drug education: A six-year multilevel analysis of project DARE," *Journal of Research in Crime and Delinquency* 35, no. 4 (1998): pp. 381–412; Christopher, Ringwalt, Susan T. Ennett, and Kathleen D. Holt, "An outcome evaluation of Project DARE (drug abuse resistance education)," *Health Education Research* 6, no. 3 (1991): pp. 327–337;

Harold K. Becker, Michael W. Agopian, and Sandy Yeh, "Impact evaluation of drug abuse resistance education (DARE)," *Journal of Drug Education* 22, no. 4 (1992): pp. 283–291; William DeJong, "A short-term evaluation of Project DARE (Drug Abuse Resistance Education): Preliminary indications of effectiveness," *Journal of Drug Education* 17, no. 4 (1987): pp. 279–294.
5. Bruce Bagley, *Drug Trafficking and Organized Crime in the Americas: Major Trends in the Twenty-Frist Century* (Washington, DC: Woodrow Wilson Center International Center for Scholars, 2012); Paul Gootenberg, *Andean cocaine: the making of a global drug* (Chapel Hill, NC: University of North Carolina Press, 2008); Bruce M. Bagley and Jonathan D. Rosen, eds., *Drug Trafficking, Organized Crime, and Violence in the Americas* Today (Gainesville, FL: University Press of Florida, 2015).
6. Bruce M. Bagley and Jonathan D. Rosen, eds., *Drug Trafficking, Organized Crime, and Violence in the Americas Today*; Frank O. Mora, "Victims of the balloon effect: Drug trafficking and US policy in Brazil and the Southern Cone of Latin America," *The Journal of Social, Political, and Economic Studies* 21, no. 2 (1996): p. 115; Matthew H. Gendle and Carmen C. Mónico, "The balloon effect: the role of US drug policy in the displacement of unaccompanied minors from the Central American northern triangle," *Journal of Trafficking, Organized Crime and Security* 3, no. 1–2 (2017): p. 12; Ralph Seccombe, "Squeezing the balloon: International drugs policy," *Drug and Alcohol Review* 14, no. 3 (1995): pp. 311–316; Liliana M. Davalos, Adriana C. Bejarano, and H. Leonardo Correa, "Disabusing cocaine: Pervasive myths and enduring realities of a globalised commodity," *International Journal of Drug Policy* 20, no. 5 (2009): pp. 381–386.
7. Kate Doyle, "The militarization of the drug war in Mexico," *Current History* 92, no. 571 (1993): p. 83; Coletta Youngers, "Cocaine Madness Counternarcotics and Militarization in the Andes," *NACLA Report on the Americas* 34, no. 3 (2000): pp. 16–23; Josiah Heyman and Howard Campbell, "The militarization of the United States-Mexico border region," *Revista de Estudos Universitários-REU* 38, no. 1 (2012): pp. 75–94; Adam Isacson, Lisa Haugaard, and Joy Olson, "Creeping militarization in the Americas," *NACLA Report on the Americas* 38, no. 3 (2004): pp. 4–7.
8. David Pion-Berlin and Miguel Carreras, "Armed forces, police and crime-fighting in Latin America," *Journal of Politics in Latin America* 9, no. 3 (2017): pp. 3–26; David Pion-Berlin and Harold Trinkunas, "Latin America's growing security gap," *Journal of Democracy* 22, no. 1 (2011): pp. 39–53.

9. Sergio Herzog, "Militarization and demilitarization processes in the Israeli and American police forces: Organizational and social aspects," *Policing and Society: An International Journal* 11, no. 2 (2001): pp. 181–208; Rut Diamint, "A new militarism in Latin America," *Journal of Democracy* 26, no. 4 (2015): pp. 155–168; Orlando J. Pérez, "Democratic legitimacy and public insecurity: Crime and democracy in El Salvador and Guatemala," *Political Science Quarterly* 118, no. 4 (2003): pp. 627–644.
10. Jonathan D. Rosen and Roberto Zepeda, *Organized Crime, Drug Trafficking, and Violence in Mexico: The Transition from Felipe Calderón to Enrique Peña Nieto*; Jonathan D. Rosen, *The Losing War: Plan Colombia and Beyond* (Albany, NY: State University of New York Press, 2014).
11. For more, see: Adam Isacson, "Confronting Colombia's Coca Boom Requires Patience and a Commitment to the Peace Accords," *WOLA*, March 13, 2017, https://www.wola.org/analysis/confronting-colombias-coca-boom-requires-patience-commitment-peace-accords/, accessed September 29, 2019.
12. Kate Swanson, "Zero tolerance in Latin America: punitive paradox in urban policy mobilities," *Urban Geography* 34, no. 7 (2013): pp. 972–988.
13. For more, see: Jonathan D. Rosen and Hanna Samir Kassab, *Drugs, Gangs, and Violence* (New York, NY: Palgrave Macmillan, 2018).
14. John Bailey and Jorge Chabat, eds. *Transnational crime and public security: challenges to Mexico and the United States* (San Diego, CA: Center for US-Mexican Studies/University of California, San Diego, 2002); Jorge Chabat, "La respuesta del gobierno de Calderón al desafío del narcotráfico: entre lo malo y lo peor," (2010), paper; Jonathan D. Rosen, Bruce Bagley, and Jorge Chabat, eds., *The Criminalization of States: The Relationship Between States and Organized Crime* (Lanham, MD: Lexington Books, 2019); Jonathan D. Rosen and Roberto Zepeda, *Organized Crime, Drug Trafficking, and Violence in Mexico: The Transition from Felipe Calderón to Enrique Peña* Nieto (Lanham, MD: Lexington Books, 2016).
15. For more, see: Miriam Gohara, "Keep on Keeping On: Maintaining Momentum for Criminal Justice Reform During the Trump Era," *Stanford Journal of Civil Rights and Civil Liberties* 14 (2018): pp.1–18; Barack Obama, "The President's Role in Advancing Criminal Justice Reform," *Harvard Law Review* 130 (2016): p. 811; Susan N. Herman, "Getting There: On Strategies for Implementing Criminal Justice Reform," *Berkeley Journal of Criminal Law* 23 (2018): pp. 32–72.
16. For more, see: José Miguel Cruz, "Central American maras: from youth street gangs to transnational protection rackets," *Global Crime* 11, no. 4 (2010): pp. 379–398.

17. Ethan Nadelmann has argued this. For more, see: Ethan A. Nadelmann, "Commonsense drug policy," *Foreign Affairs* (1998): pp. 111–126; Ethan A. Nadelmann, "Criminologists and punitive drug prohibition: To serve or to challenge?" *Criminology & Public Policy* 3, no. 3 (2004): pp. 441–450; Ethan A. Nadelmann, "Thinking seriously about alternatives to drug prohibition," *Daedalus* 121, no. 3 (1992): pp. 85–132; Ethan A. Nadelmann, "Global prohibition regimes: The evolution of norms in international society," *International Organization* 44, no. 4 (1990): pp. 479–526; Ethan A. Nadelmann, "International Drug Trafficking and US Foreign Policy," *The Washington Quarterly* 8, no. 4 (1985): 87–104.
18. Roberto Zepeda and Jonathan D. Rosen, eds., *Cooperation and Drug Policies in the Americas: Trends in the Twenty-First Century* (Lanham, MD: Lexington Books, 2014).
19. For more, see: John P. Sullivan and Robert J. Bunker, "Mexican Cartel Tactical Note# 40: Cártel Santa Rosa de Lima (CSRL) Tunnels in Guanajuato Highlights Tactical Considerations in Underground Operations," *Small Wars Journal* 22 (2019).
20. Mirjam Van Het Loo, Ineke Van Beusekom, and James P. Kahan, "Decriminalization of drug use in Portugal: the development of a policy," *The Annals of the American Academy of Political and Social Science* 582, no. 1 (2002): pp. 49–63.
21. Priscillia Hunt and Rosalie Liccardo Pacula, "Early impacts of marijuana legalization: an evaluation of prices in Colorado and Washington," *The Journal of Primary Prevention* 38, no. 3 (2017): pp. 221–248.
22. Quoted in Deirdre Walsh, "House Approves Decriminalizing Marijuana; Bill To Stall In Senate," *NPR*, December 4, 2020.
23. Deirdre Walsh, "House Approves Decriminalizing Marijuana; Bill To Stall In Senate."
24. José Miguel Cruz, Rosario Queirolo, and María Fernanda Boidi, "Determinants of public support for marijuana legalization in Uruguay, the United States, and El Salvador," *Journal of Drug Issues* 46, no. 4 (2016): pp. 308–325; José Miguel Cruz, Maria Fernanda Boidi, and Rosario Queirolo, "Saying no to weed: Public opinion towards cannabis legalisation in Uruguay," *Drugs: Education, Prevention and Policy* 25, no. 1 (2018): pp. 67–76; María Fernanda Boidi, Rosario Queirolo, and José Miguel Cruz, "Cannabis consumption patterns among frequent consumers in Uruguay," *International Journal of Drug Policy* 34 (2016): pp. 34–40.
25. Astrid Arraras and Emily D. Bello-Pardo, "Inventando Caminos: Cannabis Regulation in Uruguay," in *Cooperation and Drug Policies in the Americas Trends in the Twenty- First Century*, edited by Roberto Zepeda and

Jonathan D. Rosen (Lanham, Maryland: Lexington Books, 2014): pp. 173–197.
26. Quoted in Reuters Staff, "Mexico Supreme Court says ban on recreational marijuana unconstitutional," *Reuters*, October 31, 2018.
27. VOA News, "Mexico Takes a Step Toward Legalizing Marijuana," *VOA*, November 20, 2020.
28. For more, see: Andrés Mendiburo-Seguel, Salvador Vargas, Juan C. Oyanedel, Francisca Torres, Eduardo Vergara, and Mike Hough, "Attitudes towards drug policies in Latin America: results from a Latin-American Survey," *International Journal of Drug Policy* 41 (2017): pp. 8–13.
29. For more, see: June N.P. Francis, and Gary A. Mauser, "Collateral damage: the 'War on Drugs', and the Latin America and Caribbean region: policy recommendations for the Obama administration," *Policy Studies* 32, no. 2 (2011): pp. 159–177; Bruce M. Bagley, "Colombia and the War on Drugs," *Foreign Affairs* 67, no. 1 (1988): pp. 70–92; Jordi Cami, and Magí Farré, "Drug addiction," *New England Journal of Medicine* 349, no. 10 (2003): pp. 975–986; Eric J Nestler, "Molecular mechanisms of drug addiction," *Neuropharmacology* 47 (2004): pp. 24–32; Carl L. Hart, "Viewing addiction as a brain disease promotes social injustice," *Nature Human Behaviour* 1, no. 3 (2017): p. 1.
30. Steve Aos, Marna Miller, and Elizabeth Drake, "Evidence-based public policy options to reduce future prison construction, criminal justice costs, and crime rates," *Fed. Sent. R.* 19 (2006): p. 275; Caitlin E. Hughes, "Evidence-based policy or policy-based evidence? The role of evidence in the development and implementation of the Illicit Drug Diversion Initiative," *Drug and Alcohol Review* 26, no. 4 (2007): pp. 363–368; John Strang, Thomas Babor, Jonathan Caulkins, Benedikt Fischer, David Foxcroft, and Keith Humphreys, "Drug policy and the public good: evidence for effective interventions," *The Lancet* 379, no. 9810 (2012): pp. 71–83.

Selected Work Cited

Alexander, Michelle. *The New Jim Crow: Mass Incarceration in the Age of Colorblindness* (New York, NY: The New Press, 2010).

Allyn, Bobby. "Philadelphia Nonprofit Opening Nation's 1st Supervised Injection Site Next Week," *NPR*, February 26, 2020.

Anderson, John Lee. "The Afterlife of Pablo Escobar: In Colombia, a drug lord's posthumous celebrity brings profits and controversy," *The New Yorker*, February 26, 2018.

Applegate, Brandon K. Francis T. Cullen, Michael G. Turner, and Jody L. Sundt. "Assessing public support for three-strikes-and-you're-out laws: Global versus specific attitudes," *Crime & Delinquency* 42, no. 4 (1996): pp. 517–534.

Arraras, Astrid and Emily D. Bello-Pardo. "Inventando Caminos: Cannabis Regulation in Uruguay," in *Cooperation and Drug Policies in the Americas Trends in the Twenty-First Century*, edited by Roberto Zepeda and Jonathan D. Rosen (Lanham, Maryland: Lexington Books, 2014): pp. 173–197.

Armstrong, David. "The Family Trying to Escape Blame for the Opioid Crisis," *The Atlantic*, April 10, 2018.

Austin, James and Lauren-Brooke Eisen with James Cullen and Jonathan Frank. *How Many Americans Are Unnecessarily Incarcerated?* (New York, NY: Brennen Center for Justice, 2016).

Bagley, Bruce M. and Jonathan D. Rosen, eds. *Drug Trafficking, Organized Crime, and Violence in the Americas Today* (Gainesville, FL: University Press of Florida, 2015).

Bagley, Bruce M. ed. *Drug Trafficking Research in the Americas* (Coral Gables, FL: University of Miami, North-South Center, 1997).

Bales, William D. and Linda G. Dees. "Mandatory minimum sentencing in Florida: Past trends and future implications," *Crime & Delinquency* 38, no. 3 (1992): pp. 309–329.

Bargent, James. *Colombia's Mirror: War and Drug Trafficking in the Prison System* (Washington, DC: InSight Crime, 2017).

Barrett, Damon. "Harm reduction is not enough for supply side policy: A human rights-based approach offers more," *International Journal of Drug Policy* 23, no. 1 (2012): pp. 18–19.

Bastos, Francisco I. Waleska Caiaffa, Diana Rossi, Marcelo Vila, and Monica Malta. "The children of mama coca: Coca, cocaine and the fate of harm reduction in South America," *International Journal of Drug Policy* 18, no. 2 (2007): pp. 99–106.

Bazelon, Emily. *Charged: The New Movement to Transform American Prosecution and End Mass Incarceration* (New York, NY: Random House, 2019).

Bloom, Barbara, Barbara Owen, Elizabeth Piper Deschenes, and Jill Rosenbaum. "Moving toward justice for female juvenile offenders in the new millennium: Modeling gender-specific policies and programs," *Journal of Contemporary Criminal Justice* 18, no. 1 (2002): pp. 37–56.

Bowden, Charles. *Murder City: Ciudad Juárez and the global economy's new killing fields* (New York, NY: Nation Books, 2010).

Bowden, Charles. *Juárez: The laboratory of our future* (New York, NY: Aperture, 1998).

Brienen, Marten W. and Jonathan D. Rosen. "Introduction," in *New Approaches to Drug Policies: A Time For Change*, eds. Marten W. Brienen and Jonathan D. Rosen (New York, NY: Palgrave Macmillan, 2015): pp. 1–13

Camacho, Adriana and Daniel Mejia. "The health consequences of aerial spraying illicit crops: The case of Colombia," *Journal of Health Economics* 54 (2017): pp. 147–160.

Carpenter, Ted Galen. *The Fire Next Door: Mexico's Drug Violence and the Danger to America*, (Washington, D.C.: Cato Institute, 2012).

Nicholas Casey. "Colombia's President, Juan Manuel Santos, Is Awarded Nobel Peace Prize *The New York Times*, October 7, 2016.

Chepesiuk, Ron. *Crazy Charlie: Carlos Lehder, Revolutionary or Neo Nazi* (Rock Hill, SC: Strategic Media Books, 2016).

Coid, Jeremy W. "The Federal Administrative Maximum Penitentiary, Florence, Colorado," *Medicine, Science and the Law* 41, no. 4 (2001): pp. 287–297.

Chernick, Marc W. "Negotiated settlement to armed conflict: Lessons from the Colombian peace process," *Journal of Interamerican Studies and World Affairs* 30, no. 4 (1988): pp. 53–88.

Chernick, Marc. "The paramilitarization of the war in Colombia," *NACLA Report on the Americas* 31, no. 5 (1998): pp. 28–33.
Crandall, Russell. *Driven by Drugs* (Boulder, Colo: Lynne Rienner, 2002).
Crandall, Russell. "Explicit narcotization: US policy toward Colombia during the Samper administration," *Latin American Politics and Society* 43, no. 3 (2001): pp. 95–120.
Cruz, José Miguel. "Central American maras: from youth street gangs to transnational protection rackets," *Global Crime* 11, no. 4 (2010): pp. 379–398.
Cruz, José Miguel Rosario Queirolo, and María Fernanda Boidi. "Determinants of public support for marijuana legalization in Uruguay, the United States, and El Salvador," *Journal of Drug Issues* 46, no. 4 (2016): pp. 308–325.
Cruz, José Miguel. Jonathan D. Rosen, Luis Enrique Amaya, and Yulia Vorobyeva. *The New Face of Street Gangs: The Gang Phenomenon in El Salvador* (Miami, FL: FIU, 2017).
Dal Bó, Ernesto, Pedro Dal Bó, and Rafael Di Tella. "'Plata o Plomo?': bribe and punishment in a theory of political influence," *American Political Science Review* 100, no. 1 (2006): pp. 41–53.
Davalos, Liliana M. Adriana C. Bejarano, and H. Leonardo Correa. "Disabusing cocaine: Pervasive myths and enduring realities of a globalised commodity," *International Journal of Drug Policy* 20, no. 5 (2009): pp. 381–386.
Department of Justice (DOJ). "Fourteen Individuals Charged for Operating 'Pill Mills' and Illegally Prescribing Drugs to Hundreds of Patients in Multiple Locations in the Philadelphia Area," *DOJ*, February 6, 2019.
Drug Enforcement Administration (DEA). *Colombian Cocaine Production Expansion Contributes to Rise in Supply in the United States* (Springfield, VA: DEA, 2017).
Delacour, Justin. "Plan Colombia: Rhetoric, Reality, and the Press," *Social Justice* 27, no. 4 82 (2000): pp. 63–75.
DeJong, William. "A short-term evaluation of Project DARE (Drug Abuse Resistance Education): Preliminary indications of effectiveness," *Journal of Drug Education* 17, no. 4 (1987): pp. 279–294.
Fagan, Jeffrey. "Women and drugs revisited: Female participation in the cocaine economy," *Journal of Drug Issues* 24, no. 2 (1994): pp. 179–225.
Farrington, David P. and Christopher P. Nuttall. "Prison size, overcrowding, prison violence, and recidivism," *Journal of Criminal Justice* 8, no. 4 (1980): pp. 221–231.
Fields, Gary. "White House Czar Calls for End to 'War on Drugs,'" *The Wall Street Journal*, May 14, 2009.
Filippone, Robert. "The Medellin Cartel: Why we can't win the drug war," *Studies in Conflict & Terrorism* 17, no. 4 (1994): pp. 323–344.

Foltin, Richard W. Amie S. Ward, Margaret Haney, Carl L. Hart, and Eric D. Collins. "The effects of escalating doses of smoked cocaine in humans," *Drug and Alcohol Dependence* 70, no. 2 (2003): pp. 149–157.

Ford, Matt. "Jeff Sessions Reinvigorates the Drug War," *The Atlantic*, May 12, 2017; Department of Justice (DOJ), Justice Department Issues Memo on Marijuana Enforcement, *DOJ*, https://www.justice.gov/opa/pr/justice-department-issues-memo-marijuana-enforcement, January 4, 2018, accessed June 29, 2020.

Francis, June N.P. and Gary A. Mauser. "Collateral damage: the 'War on Drugs', and the Latin America and Caribbean region: policy recommendations for the Obama administration," *Policy Studies* 32, no. 2 (2011): pp. 159–177.

Friedman, Matthew, Ames C. Grawert, and James Cullen. *Crime Trends: 1990–2016* (New York, NY: Brennan Center for Justice, 2017).

Gillespie, Wayne. "A multilevel model of drug abuse inside prison," *The Prison Journal* 85, no. 2 (2005): pp. 223–246.

Goldstein, Avram and Harold Kalant. "Drug policy: striking the right balance," *Science* 249, no. 4976 (1990): pp. 1513–1521.

Gootenberg, Paul. *Andean Cocaine: The Making of a Global Drug* (Chapel Hill, NC: University of North Carolina Press, 2008).

Hart, Carl L. Mark Haney, R. W. Foltin, and M. W. Fischman. "Alternative reinforcers differentially modify cocaine self-administration by humans," *Behavioural Pharmacology* 11, no. 1 (2000): pp. 87–91.

Hart, Carl L. Margaret Haney, Suzanne K. Vosburg, Eric Rubin, and Richard W. Foltin. "Smoked cocaine self-administration is decreased by modafinil," *Neuropsychopharmacology* 33, no. 4 (2008): pp. 761–768.

Hawdon, James E. "The role of presidential rhetoric in the creation of a moral panic: Reagan, Bush, and the war on drugs," *Deviant Behavior* 22, no. 5 (2001): pp. 419–445.

Herman, Susan N. "Getting There: On Strategies for Implementing Criminal Justice Reform," *Berkeley Journal of Criminal Law* 23 (2018): pp. 32–72.

Hunt, Priscillia and Rosalie Liccardo Pacula. "Early impacts of marijuana legalization: an evaluation of prices in Colorado and Washington," *The Journal of Primary Prevention* 38, no. 3 (2017): pp. 221–248.

Hughes, Caitlin E. "Evidence-based policy or policy-based evidence? The role of evidence in the development and implementation of the Illicit Drug Diversion Initiative," *Drug and Alcohol Review* 26, no. 4 (2007): pp. 363–368

Isacson, Adam, Lisa Haugaard, and Joy Olson. "Creeping militarization in the Americas," *NACLA Report on the Americas* 38, no. 3 (2004): pp. 4–7.

Isacson, Adam. "Making Sense of Colombia's 'Post-Conflict' Conflict," in *The Criminalization of State: The Relationship between States and Organized Crime*, eds. Jonathan D. Rosen, Bruce Bagley, and Jorge Chabat (Lanham, MD: Lexington Books, 2019), pp. 209–227.

Kassab, Hanna S. and Jonathan D. Rosen, eds. *Violence in the Americas* (Lanham, MD: Lexington Books, 2018).

Krebs, Christopher P. Michael Costelloe, and David Jenks. "Drug control policy and smuggling innovation: a game-theoretic analysis," *Journal of Drug Issues* 33, no. 1 (2003): pp. 133–160.

Lander, María Fernanda. "La voz impenitente de la 'sicaresca' colombiana," *Revista Iberoamericana* 73, no. 218 (2007): pp. 287–299.

Lankenau, Stephen E. "Smoke'em if you got'em: Cigarette black markets in US prisons and jails," *The Prison Journal* 81, no. 2 (2001): pp. 142–161.

Lat, David. "How Tough-on-Crime Prosecutors Contribute to Mass Incarceration," *The New York Times*, April 8, 2019.

Lee, Rensselaer W. "Cocaine mafia," *Society* 27, no. 2 (1990): pp. 53–62.

Lessing, Benjamin. "Logics of violence in criminal war," *Journal of Conflict Resolution* 59, no. 8 (2015): 1486–1516.

Lessing, Benjamin. *Making Peace in Drug Wars: Crackdowns and Cartels in Latin America* (New York, NY: Cambridge University Press, 2018).

LeoGrande William M. and Kenneth E. Sharpe. "Two Wars or One? Drugs, Guerrillas, and Colombia's New 'Violencia,'" *World Policy Journal* 17, no. 3 (2000): pp. 1–11.

Molano, Alfredo. "The Evolution of the FARC: A guerrilla group's long history," *NACLA Report on the Americas* 34, no. 2 (2000): pp. 23–31.

Mueller, Robert S. "Mandatory minimum sentencing," *Federal Sentencing Reporter* 4, no. 4 (1992): pp. 230–233.

Nadelmann, Ethan A. "Thinking Seriously about Alternatives to Drug Prohibition," *Daedalus* 121, no. 31 (1992): pp. 85–85.

Naef, Patrick. "'Narco-heritage' and the Touristification of the Drug Lord Pablo Escobar in Medellín, Colombia," *Journal of Anthropological Research* 74, no. 4 (2018): pp. 485–502.

National Drug Intelligence Center U.S. Department of Justice (NDIC), *Drug Market Analysis: Philadelphia/Camden High Intensity Drug Trafficking Area* (Washington, DC: NDIC, 2008).

Nussio, Enzo and Kimberly Howe. "What if the FARC Demobilizes?" *Stability: International Journal of Security & Development* 1, no. 1 (2012): pp. 58–67.

Oehme, Chester G. "Plan Colombia: reassessing the strategic framework," *Democracy and Security* 6, no. 3 (2010): pp. 221–236.

Osorio, Javier. "The contagion of drug violence: spatiotemporal dynamics of the Mexican war on drugs," *Journal of Conflict Resolution* 59, no. 8 (2015): pp. 1403–1432.

Osorio, Javier and Alejandro Reyes. "Supervised event coding from text written in Spanish: Introducing eventus id," *Social Science Computer Review* 35, no. 3 (2017): pp. 406–416.

Parra, Michael W. and José Mauricio Suárez-Becerra. "Twenty Years after the Killing of the King of Kingpins Pablo Escobar: Lessons Learned from Narco-Terrorism," *Journal Trauma Treatment* 1, no. 113 (2012): pp. 1–2.

Perkinson, Robert. "Shackled justice: Florence Federal Penitentiary and the new politics of punishment," *Social Justice* 21, no. 3 (57) (1994): pp. 117–132.

Pérez, Orlando J. "Democratic legitimacy and public insecurity: Crime and democracy in El Salvador and Guatemala," *Political Science Quarterly* 118, no. 4 (2003): pp. 627–644.

Pérez Ricart, Carlos A. "The Role of the DEA in the Emergence of the Field of Anti-narcotics Policing in Latin America," *Global Governance: A Review of Multilateralism and International Organizations* 24, no. 2 (2018): pp. 169–192.

Perrone, Dina and Travis C. Pratt. "Comparing the quality of confinement and cost-effectiveness of public versus private prisons: What we know, why we do not know more, and where to go from here," *The Prison Journal* 83, no. 3 (2003): pp. 301–322.

Pion-Berlin, David and Harold Trinkunas. "Latin America's growing security gap," *Journal of Democracy* 22, no. 1 (2011): pp. 39–53.

Podolsky, Scott H. David Herzberg, and Jeremy A. Greene. "Preying on Prescribers (and Their Patients)—Pharmaceutical Marketing, Iatrogenic Epidemics, and the Sackler Legacy," *New England Journal of Medicine* 380, no. 19 (2019): pp. 1785–1787.

Poveda, Tony G. "Clinton, crime, and the justice department," *Social Justice* 21, no. 3 57 (1994): pp. 73–84.

Pratt, Travis C. and Jeff Maahs. "Are private prisons more cost-effective than public prisons? A meta-analysis of evaluation research studies," *Crime & Delinquency* 45, no. 3 (1999): pp. 358–371.

Restrepo, Elvira Maria, Fabio Sánchez, and Mariana Martínez Cuéllar. "Impunity or punishment? An analysis of criminal investigation into kidnapping, terrorism and embezzlement in Colombia," *Global Crime* 7, no. 2 (2006): pp. 176–199.

Roberts, John and Evan Wright. *American Desperado: My Life--From Mafia Soldier to Cocaine Cowboy to Secret Government Asset* (New York, NY: Broadway Paperbacks, 2011).

Rosen, Jonathan D. and Roberto Zepeda. *Organized Crime, Drug Trafficking, and Violence in Mexico: The Transition from Felipe Calderón to Enrique Peña Nieto* (Lanham, MD: Lexington Books, 2016).

Schwab, Tim. "US opioid prescribing: the federal government advisers with recent ties to big pharma," *Bmj* 366 (2019): pp. l5167.

Stokes, Doug. "Better lead than bread? A critical analysis of the US's plan Colombia," *Civil Wars* 4, no. 2 (2001): pp. 59–78.

Strang, John, Thomas Babor, Jonathan Caulkins, Benedikt Fischer, David Foxcroft, and Keith Humphreys. "Drug policy and the public good: evidence for effective interventions," *The Lancet* 379, no. 9810 (2012): pp. 71–83.

The Sentencing Project. *Fact Sheet: Trends in U.S. Corrections* (Washington, DC: The Sentencing Project, 2019).

Tate, Winifred. "US human rights activism and plan Colombia," *Colombia Internacional* 69 (2009): pp. 50–69.

Tickner, Arlene B. Laura Alonso, Lara Loaiza, Natalia Suárez, Diana Castellanos, and Juan Diego Cárdenas. *Women and Organized Crime in Latin America: beyond victims or victimizers* (Bogotá, CO: El Observatorio Colombiano de Crimen Organizado and InSight Crime, 2020).

Thomas, Ellen S. "Plea bargaining: The clash between theory and practice," *Loyola Law Review* 20 (1973): pp. 303–312.

Toro, María Celia. "The internationalization of police: The DEA in Mexico," *The Journal of American History* 86, no. 2 (1999): pp. 623–640.

United Nations Offices on Drugs and Crime (UNODC). Colombia: Coca cultivation survey 2009 (Bogotá, CO: UNODC, 2010).

Vaicius, Ingrid and Adam Isacson. "The 'war on drugs' meets the 'war on terror,'" *International Policy Report* 2, no. 6 (2003): pp. 1–27.

Van Het Loo, Mirjam, Ineke Van Beusekom, and James P. Kahan. "Decriminalization of drug use in Portugal: the development of a policy," *The Annals of the American Academy of Political and Social Science* 582, no. 1 (2002): pp. 49–63.

Visher, Christy A. Sara A. Debus-Sherrill, and Jennifer Yahner. "Employment after prison: A longitudinal study of former prisoners," *Justice Quarterly* 28, no. 5 (2011): pp. 698–718.

Washington Office on Latin America (WOLA). "Colombia Pushes Coca Eradication During COVID-19 Pandemic," *WOLA*, April 23, 2020, https://www.wola.org/2020/04/colombia-covid19-coca-eradication/, accessed May 15, 2020.

Werb, Daniel, Adeeba Kamarulzaman, M. C. Meacham, Claudio Rafful, Benedikt Fischer, S. A. Strathdee, and Evan Wood. "The effectiveness of compulsory drug treatment: a systematic review," *International Journal of Drug Policy* 28 (2016): pp. 1–9.

Whelan, Aubrey. "How Philly plans to combat the nation's worst big-city opioid crisis in 2020," *Philadelphia Inquirer*, January 21, 2020.

White, Christopher M. *The War on Drugs in the Americas* (New York, NY: Routledge, 2019).

Whynes, David. "Illicit Drug Production and Supply-side Drugs Policy in Asia and South America," *Development and Change* 22, no. 3 (1991): pp. 475–496.

Youngers, Coletta. "Cocaine Madness Counternarcotics and Militarization in the Andes," *NACLA Report on the Americas* 34, no. 3 (2000): pp. 16–23.

Young Vernetta D. and Rebecca Reviere. *Women Behind Bars: Gender and Race in US prisons* (Boulder, CO: Lynne Rienner Publishers, 2006).

Zepeda, Roberto and Jonathan D. Rosen, eds. *Cooperation and Drug Policies in the Americas: Trends in the Twenty-First Century* (Lanham, MD: Lexington Books, December 2014).

Index[1]

A
Abroad, 1, 3, 5, 7, 97–114, 125, 127, 130
Academics, 7, 8, 63, 109, 123, 124, 126, 130
Addiction, 8, 10, 75–89, 104, 106, 107, 114, 123, 128, 130
Advocates, 5, 6, 86, 104, 105, 125, 128, 129
Americas, 7, 10, 11n2, 24, 97, 98, 109–112, 124–126, 129, 130
Andean Information Network (AIN), 110
Ayotzinapa, 56

B
Beltrán Leyva Organization, 46, 52, 54, 56
Biodiversity, 25

Blanco, Griselda, 18, 19
Boggs Act, 3
Bogotá, 21, 24
Bush, George W., 5, 9, 23, 24, 88

C
Cali cartel, 9, 20–22, 52
Cannabis, 129
Central America through the Central America Regional Security Initiative (CARSI), 51
Chabat, Jorge, 47, 126
Chernick, Marc, 30
Clinton, Bill, 4, 5, 9, 23, 99, 100, 105
Coca, 5, 9, 18, 23, 25–28, 32–35, 63, 123, 124
Cocaine, 3, 4, 8, 9, 18–20, 25–26, 29, 30, 32, 34–36, 45, 52, 81, 83, 84, 103, 104, 110, 111, 124, 125

---

[1] Note: Page numbers followed by 'n' refer to notes.

146   INDEX

Colorado, 6, 21, 128
Córdoba, 28
Coronavirus, 35, 64, 88
Corruption, 9, 10, 21, 23, 24, 34, 36, 46, 48–50, 53–59, 62–66, 125–127
Criminal bands, 9, 28–30

D
Democracy, 9, 24, 46, 49, 58, 65
Doctors, 10, 47, 76–79, 89
Domestic violence, 110, 113
Drug Abuse Resistance Education (DARE), 124
Drug Enforcement Administration (DEA), 3, 22, 29, 47, 78, 129
Dudley, Steven, 111

E
El Salvador, 111, 112, 114, 126, 127
Epidemic, 3, 4, 10, 75, 76, 78, 80, 86, 89, 123
Escape, 57, 58, 66
Escobar, Pablo, 17, 20–22, 36
Evidence, 34, 56, 103, 130

F
Farmers, 25, 26, 34, 35, 62, 63, 124
Federal prison, 2, 6, 45, 47, 78, 100, 102, 110
Fentanyl, 10, 75–89
Foreign policy, 5, 7, 23
Fox, Vicente, 49
Fragmentation, 8, 9, 22, 27, 47, 51, 52
Fresno, California, 98

G
Gang, 27, 56, 63, 83–85, 100, 109, 111, 112
Globalization, 35, 48, 124, 128
Griffin, Teresa, 104
Guerrero, 55–57, 62–64, 66
Guerrero-Gutiérrez, Eduardo, 51

H
Harrison Narcotics Tax Act of 1914, 3
Havana, Cuba, 30
Herbicides, 23, 25, 34
HIV/AIDS, 128
Homicides, 19, 26, 27, 36, 53, 83, 84
Human rights, 28–30, 35, 46, 57, 61, 114

I
Illicit economies, 110
Impunity, 9, 10, 24, 34, 36, 47–50, 53, 60, 63–65, 126–127
Isacson, Adam, 26, 34

J
Journalist, 21, 53, 56, 61, 130
Juárez cartel, 54
Judges, 20, 21, 36, 85, 105, 108, 110, 126, 127
Jungle, 26
Justice, 7, 21, 56, 65, 97–99, 102, 106, 109, 110, 113, 114, 130
Justice reform, 104, 130
Juvenile, 108

K

Kensington, 10, 82–84, 86
Kidnappings, 21, 27, 56, 99
Kilograms, 62, 110
Knights Templar, 51

L

Latin America, 10, 98, 109–112, 125, 127
Latin American Public Opinion Project (LAPOP), 31, 33, 57, 58, 60, 65
Lessing, Benjamin, 47
Life sentence, 47, 84, 100, 102–104
Los Angeles, 98, 126

M

Marijuana, 2, 3, 6, 18, 20, 46, 128, 129
Mayor, 53, 56, 84, 126
Medellín cartel, 17–22, 52
Mérida Initiative, 8, 9, 49–51, 54, 69n23, 125, 130
Metric tons, 32, 62
Miami, 9, 17–19, 77, 82
Michoacán, 49, 55, 63, 64, 66
Middle East, 24
Militarized, 23, 50, 61, 66
Montoya, Diego, 29
MORENA party, 59, 60
Mountains, 26, 62, 63
MS-13, 27, 111, 127

N

National emergency, 123
National Guard, 61, 66
New York, 18, 19, 30, 52, 82, 83, 100, 104, 126

New York City, 76, 126
Nixon, Richard, 1, 3

O

Obama, Barack, 5, 6, 51, 88, 104
Office of National Drug Control Policy (ONDCP), 23
Opium, 46, 62–64
Oranges, 26, 106
Overdoses, 4, 75, 77, 79, 81, 85, 89, 107
OxyContin, 76–81

P

Pakistan, 23
Peña Nieto, Enrique, 9, 46, 54–59, 66
Philadelphia, 10, 75, 81–86, 107
Plan Colombia, 5, 8, 9, 18, 22–25, 27, 28, 36, 49, 50, 125, 130
Police, 2, 19–23, 28, 35, 36, 49–51, 53, 54, 56, 61–66, 77, 83, 99, 104, 105, 107, 111, 125–127
Politicians, 4, 53, 59, 62, 65, 98, 99, 109, 112, 113, 124, 127, 130
Prescriptions, 78, 79, 83, 89
Prosecutorial discretion, 108
Purdue Pharma, 76

Q

Quintero, Rafael Caro, 47

R

Race, 102–105
Reagan, Ronald, 4
Recovery, 81, 82, 85

Reforms, 6, 9, 10, 36, 46, 49, 50, 53, 54, 56, 58, 61, 64–66, 105, 108, 113, 114, 125–127
Reynolds, Mike, 98, 99

S
Sackler family, 76, 77
Safe injection sites, 75, 85–86
San Pedro Sula, Honduras, 126
Santos, Juan Manuel, 18, 30–34
Science, 7, 10, 81, 123, 124, 130
Senate, 60, 63, 129
Sessions, Jeff, 6
Sinaloa cartel, 51–54, 57, 58, 61, 64, 128
Southern District of New York, 30
Southwest border, 62, 88
Stigma, 82
Supreme Court, 6, 129
Switzerland, 23

T
Tijuana cartel, 51
Tough on crime, 2, 4, 9, 10, 97–114, 127
Transit, 8, 128, 129
Trump, Donald, 6, 7, 9, 10, 33, 34, 36, 76, 87, 88, 124, 128
Tug Valley, 77

U
United Nations High Commissioner for Human Rights, 56
United States House of Representatives, 129
Uribe, Álvaro, 9, 18, 23–26, 28–30, 33, 36
U.S. Department of State, 30

V
Valdez Villarreal, Edgar, 45
Victims, 22, 27, 33, 60, 61, 83, 99, 102, 111
Violence, 5, 7–10, 18, 20–22, 32, 46, 48, 52–61, 63–66, 82–84, 98, 100–102, 109–114, 125, 126

W
Wainwright, Tom, 52
Wall, 10, 76, 87–89, 112, 128
Walmart, 52
Washington, D.C., 6, 18, 83, 98, 124, 128
Women, 10, 18, 53, 99, 102–105, 110–114
World Health Organization, 32, 124

Y
Youth, 50, 108

Z
Zepeda, Roberto, 47, 126, 128
Zetas, 54, 64

Printed in the United States
by Baker & Taylor Publisher Services